THE SMART DIVORCE

THE SMART DIVORCE

SUSAN T. GOLDSTEIN AND VALERIE H. COLB

Golden Books
NEW YORK

To my parents, Frank and Henny,
for always encouraging me to be my own person and giving me
the confidence to pursue my dreams.

S. T. G.

To my husband, Jim,
who gives me unwavering support; to my parents,
Eleanor and Ben, whose love for each other
has been my inspiration; and to the memory of
Charles Oscar Aschmann, my mentor.

V. H. C.

Golden Books®
888 Seventh Avenue
New York, NY 10106

This book is not intended to be a substitute for professional legal advice.
The reader is advised to consult with an attorney before taking legal
action in marital or any other matters.

Designed by Gwen Petruska-Gürkan

Manufactured in the United States of America
10 9 8 7 6 5 4 3 2 1

Library of Congress Cataloging-in-Publication Data
Goldstein, Susan T.
    The smart divorce : a practical guide to the 200 things you must know /
Susan T. Goldstein and Valerie H. Colb.
        p.   cm.
    ISBN 1-58238-047-3
    1. Divorce—United States—Psychological aspects—Handbooks, man-
uals, etc.   2. Divorce—Law and legislation—United States—Handbooks,
manuals, etc.   I. Colb, Valerie H.   II. Title.
    HQ834.G663 1999
    306.89—dc21
                                                            98-48031
                                                            CIP

CONTENTS

INTRODUCTION

Divorce is like a head-on collision. Shock and trauma are inevitable. As Bette Davis said, "Fasten your seatbelts. It's going to be a bumpy night." Consider this book your seatbelt. We can't prevent the accident, but we can cushion the blow.

If divorce is imminent, you'll need good advice. And the best time to get the advice is *before* the process starts. *Before* you make an irrevocable mistake. *Before* you spend time worrying and suffering heartache about a "problem" that isn't a problem. *Before* you say words that can never be taken back. *Before* you burn bridges you may later want to cross.

Getting divorced is a lot like riding a roller coaster. Ups, downs, smooth patches, and then that exploding feeling that your stomach is upside down. If the adverse effects remained limited to your stomach, that would be great. But they don't. Your heart, your head, your spirit are all in for a ride that will traverse a range of emotions as diverse as sadness, anger, rejection, disillusion, relief, loss, fear, rage, despair, and abandonment.

We've written this book as your safeguard to prepare you for the roller coaster experience. With more than forty years of combined experience in practicing divorce law in Los Angeles and as two people who have lived through the divorce process personally, we bring you professional and personal knowledge of what you need to know before embarking on your divorce.

Plan ahead. Take precautions. Be prepared. You've followed those principles in every important undertaking in your life. Why wouldn't you do the same with your divorce?

After listening to hundreds of clients, we've observed that most people make mistakes that run the gamut from minor to disastrous. Why? Because they don't know any better. Because they are on a terrifying ride in unfamiliar territory.

We've written this book to give you directions and to prepare you for

- what you can expect to happen;
- what actions you can take to protect yourself;
- deciding whom you should trust;
- learning how to prioritize;
- what you must avoid;
- the practical steps to take for financial security;
- the reality of divorce and its perceived misconceptions;
- selecting the right attorney for your case;
- moving forward in the most effective fashion;
- avoiding a costly, hostile fight;
- determining if mediators and therapists should play a role in your divorce;
- stabilizing your life and your children's lives.

Without this information you will be lost. It's hard to think rationally when your world is falling apart. What do we mean? Imagine what we thought when the following occurred:

- We received a telephone call from opposing counsel advising us that our client had grabbed an ax and was in the process of chopping all the parties' furniture into kindling for the fireplace.
- Our client's wife, during her visitation time with the parties' daughters, abducted the children and disappeared with them to New Zealand.
- Our client's former husband, a middle-aged entrepreneur in the rubbish business, announced that he could no

longer support our client and their children because he was following his dream of becoming an opera singer.

- A young woman came to us and said, "I want to get a divorce, but my husband says he'll shoot the balls off my lawyer." We announced without hesitation, "We're perfect for the job."

- A famous television actor burst into tears in our office when served with divorce papers because his wife could no longer tolerate his alcoholism.

- One client found her husband in bed with another man, and before doing anything else, she immediately called the other man's wife and referred her to us.

- Our client was told by the judge what his child and spousal support would be. He stood up, outraged, and blurted out, "That's not fair! My wife and children can't live on that."

- While waiting for a hearing, we watched in shock and amazement as our client and the husband she had been divorcing went under the seats in the courtroom and began making out. Our opposing counsel agreed to a continuance while we jointly tried to shield our clients from view.

Remember when you were a kid? One minute you're holding a pile of sand in the palm of your hand, and the next instant it's gone. In the blink of an eye, sifting through the space between your fingers. Can love vanish like that? It's hard to say. All we know is that vows that said "forever" can seem a long time ago when one or both of you wants out. It would have made our ancestors blanch, but the reality is that anyone who wants out can get out.

The worst day of your life may be the day you come to terms with the reality that your marriage is over. Something you thought was forever, entered into on what may have been the happiest day of your life, has disappeared like smoke diffusing into the air.

Perhaps even more mystifying than the often-asked questions, "What went wrong? Why didn't it work?" are the less-often-asked questions, "What have I turned into? Who is this person I'm married to?"

• • •

valerie's story

Although I was only twenty-eight years old, I had already been a Beverly Hills family law attorney for five years when I married my first husband. I continued practicing family law during my marriage and opened my own law firm. Some trial lawyers whom I saw almost every week in court said they counted the years by my pregnancies. "Your youngest is two? Do you remember the case we had when you were pregnant with your first? My God, it seems like yesterday." It was difficult successfully juggling a full-time, high-end divorce practice with the responsibilities of motherhood. Although I was married, my situation gave me insight into the plight of single working parents.

During more than twenty years of practicing family law in Beverly Hills and La Cañada, California, I have represented some high-profile clients, a few clients who had truly friendly and peaceful divorces, many clients who overcame problems, and one case that ended in murder. I have settled many cases, and tried the ones I couldn't settle. I literally have lived through hundreds of divorces.

My experience helped me live through my divorce—which was protracted and difficult, sometimes bitter, frequently disappointing, and occasionally shocking. As my divorce went on, I learned why our marriage could not have continued. Perhaps I should have figured that out sooner. I am satisfied that I ever figured it out. The best thing I did for myself was set one goal for my divorce: "Learn from your mistakes. Accept that you will make different mistakes, but do not make the same mistakes again." I feel I have accomplished that. I have remarried, I have a wonderful husband and family, and those lawyers are still counting my pregnancies.

Not only did I learn about marriage from my divorce, but I also got insight about the divorce process from the inside. I had to choose a lawyer. I had to pay a lawyer. I had to appear in court and listen to a judge decide issues about our children, after mental health professionals, who were complete strangers, had passed judgment on our respective parenting skills. I realized that a particular issue, such as who gets Aunt Hilda's picture, may seem critical while you are going through your divorce, but later, when you are outside the emotional turmoil, it is only a source of amusement. Other issues, such as those about children, can be resolved successfully only if both parents look at the needs of the children and put their own needs aside. No court order can make a child love you less or want to be with you more. I became more sensitized to the difficulty of remaining calm while waiting for the truth to emerge. But because I was intimately familiar with the system, I had a sense of security and order. I knew what to expect next and how to plan for it. We want to give our readers the opportunity to have that sense of security, which is the best way to reduce stress and endure the vagaries of divorce.

• • •

susan's story

I have practiced family law in Beverly Hills since 1979. I have seen such a diverse and extraordinary range of human behavior that it is not surprising a screenwriter I was representing commented, "If I sat in your office for one week, I'd have enough material for a lifetime."

The one thing I can say with certainty is that after so many years engaged in this practice, no aspect of the human condition and behavior can shock me. On the other hand, I have never lost the capacity to be disappointed, saddened, and occasionally happily surprised.

I was lucky. Not everyone is. The lesson of my divorce is one from which others can learn. My husband and I had a cordial, equitable parting, with no animosity or ugliness. Even in divorce it's not impossible to find some common goals.

While recognizing that we wanted to end the marriage, neither my husband nor I lost sight of the fact that we still respected each other and wanted to act with integrity. Instead of operating on the principle of "What do I want?" and "How much can I get?" we both considered what would be fair. We were sensitive to the need to compromise and the importance of addressing what the other wanted. After all, we were dividing "stuff." Stuff can be replaced.

It was the saddest experience of my life, one from which I thought I would not recover. I am gratified that we could attain a different level of love and respect in parting. The failure of our marriage never made us lose sight of the good qualities that had drawn us together.

The passage of time has shown me that you don't forget the hurt, but you do heal. Time helps us come to peace with our sorrows.

*   *   *

Divorce brings out our capacity to hurt one another. If you've known how to love, you know how to hurt.

Every divorce case is a microcosm of life. Each case has a life of its own. There is always an essential conflict that causes the final, irreparable breakdown. The nature and acerbity of that conflict generally determine the tenor of the divorce. People's divorces usually reflect their marriages: Couples with a tumultuous marriage do not have a serene and peaceful divorce. Would you expect Marge and Al Bundy to have an amicable divorce? Also, a marriage that may look like the all-American dream to outsiders, frequently is not. Ken and Barbie have secrets that would astonish you.

There are certain things that most divorces have in common. We know this from our clients and having lived through the experience ourselves.

We've written this book to give you options and avenues. Pick what is applicable to *your* situation. No two divorces are the same.

When starting a divorce, an initial problem confronting you is a concern or even a fear of what the long-term ramifications will be. Apprehension about your children, your financial future, fears of loneliness, sense of failure, and the loss of things that seemed integral to your day-to-day life—it's enough to make you think long and hard before jumping into an overwhelming and bewildering process.

This book is to educate you about what are and are not realistic concerns, pierce misconceptions you may have about the process, and give pragmatic and, we hope, comforting advice about how to deal with the panic that seizes you and holds on tighter than a vise.

What about all the options out there? How will you select an attorney? Do you need therapy? Do your children? Should you consider mediation? Where do you begin to get the answers to these questions? All are best answered before you've taken the plunge.

Do you think you've considered every issue and aspect of divorce? It's unlikely. Flip through this book. We bet you will discover information that you might otherwise have overlooked. You're not in a position emotionally or professionally to think of everything.

It's hard to think rationally when you're worried that your alimony payment will equal the national debt. It's almost impossible to sleep when you know that your spouse has a loaded .45 and is truly unhappy about the idea of divorce. It's very stressful to consider pulling your child out of private school in the middle of the semester because you are overdrawn on your checking account.

We've considered all the questions that may plague you, and have tried to provide some useful and practical answers. Rest assured—you're not alone; you're not the first person to need answers to these questions. Most important, your questions won't go unanswered.

So if the end of your marriage is truly here and the time has come for you to "face the music," take our advice with you. We've written this book to be the best thing you can have, next to your best friend. And remember, even your best friend is not the best source for *certain* advice. Your best friend may tell you what you want to hear. Contained in this book is what you need to know; sometimes painful, but more often comforting and valuable. Comforting, because armed with the knowledge of what's ahead and how to deal with the system, you'll have confidence in yourself and in your future. Valuable, because "forewarned is forearmed." What is frightening is the unknown, a cold, imposing process that renders you helpless. Information gives power. This book will give you the information you need as you step into the maelstrom of divorce.

Remember that keeping a sense of humor and perspective is

often the best way to get through a trying time. We both know that sometimes we laugh so that we don't cry. There's a tried-and-true lawyer joke that goes like this:

"Honey, I want to get you a wonderful birthday present. Would you like a two-carat diamond ring with a platinum band?"

"No."

"Darling, would you like a brand-new Mercedes Benz, top of the line?"

"No."

"Sweetie, would you like a new home with five bedrooms, six bathrooms, and a three-car garage?

"No."

"Well, what would you like for your birthday?"

"A divorce."

"A divorce? No way. I didn't plan to spend *that* much!"

Keep in mind that divorce doesn't have to result in financial disaster for you and a windfall for lawyers. It will disrupt your family, but it doesn't have to destroy it. It may knock the wind out of your sails, but it doesn't have to sink the ship.

With a little luck and sound guidance, you're going to do just fine!

1

FEARS

My World Is Empty Without You

I won't have the money to do the things I used to do with friends.

Divorce is synonymous with change. Reconcile yourself: You may not be able to afford all of the things from the past.

Luxuries are the first to go when there is an economic pinch. Try to set aside money and save for some self-indulgence. It is important and healthy to have something to look forward to, whether it is a nice dinner, a weekend away, or some other pleasure. Don't forget to check newspapers and magazines for specials or coupons that may allow you to enjoy special events at reduced rates. Certain jobs come with free or reduced-rate travel privileges. Look into it.

You may be embarrassed at the loss of your country club membership, but there are worse woes in life. You'll live through it, and your true friends will stand by you.

My children won't love me anymore.

Yes, they will.

Naturally they may be confused, scared, and anxious, but as long as you give them love, you'll get it back. Divorce is a time of great emotional turmoil for everyone, but especially for you. Make an extra effort to keep as much love, understanding, and normalcy in your relationship with your children.

The two people they love the most are splitting up, frequently with conflict ranging from mild to atomic. Children need time to adjust to changes, as routine or traumatic as a move, new schedules, new home, new schools, new friends, loss of activities, and not having both parents in the same household. Children's reactions run the gamut from blaming you for the disruption to their security to being angry. Don't be surprised if they "act out." However, they will still love you and may understand you better than you expect.

Your children need more from you now than they have in the past. Be there for them. Eventually things will stabilize. Your children will survive and return the love you have offered them. Your children don't give up on you as easily as you may imagine.

My parents will think I'm a failure.

That's their problem, not yours.

The decision to end a marriage is a hard one, but it's yours alone. You have to do what's right for you, not what's right for anyone else. You're not a child.

Your parents may be disappointed that you're getting divorced, but after the initial shock, most parents will support you in any way they can.

The father of a client was delighted to learn of the divorce even though her husband was his business partner. He confided in his daughter that her husband had been stealing from the family business. After being sued by his former father-in-law, the son-in-law sheepishly settled and paid back the stolen money.

It's always tough to feel that you've let your parents down, but that's no reason to stay in a marriage that is causing you unhappiness. Explain it to them. They'll make the adjustment. Some parents make the adjustment slowly, while others take less time than anticipated. Some may even be overjoyed. Remember, our parents love us just as we love our children. What's important is *realizing* that divorce does not make you a failure.

I'll have to move.

You may have to do just that, so start changing the way you think. If your home is beyond your new budget, you're going to have to make a change. Remember, if you stay, you must be able to pay not only the mortgage but also the taxes, insurance, and maintenance. But if you rent, you must be able to afford the current rent as well as the increases that will inevitably follow. If your budget can handle it, you may be one of the fortunate ones who doesn't have to relocate.

If you're not so fortunate, instead of thinking about what you're losing, try a different focus. Think about the adventure of exploring a new neighborhood, meeting new people, seeing new scenery, and fixing up a new place. If that still doesn't appeal to you, cry for a short while, then pack your bags and get moving. There are worse things in life.

I won't have any credit.

Instead of worrying, do something about it. It's the age of the credit card, and credit is sometimes no harder to get than taking an extra five minutes to fill out an application.

Apply for gasoline credit cards in your name only. They are usually easy to obtain. Go to a few department stores and do the same. The added bonus is that some of them will even discount your purchases on that day simply because you applied for credit.

Many banks and financial institutions have their own Visa and MasterCard credit cards. Often it is only necessary to open a relatively minimal account to make you eligible for one. Once you have two or three cards, it becomes easier to get more. Watch out; it's the old story of be careful what you wish for. Credit cards are easier to obtain than to pay.

Develop a relationship with one bank. Get to know one or two of the bank officers. Make inquiries as to what they want to see if they were to give you a loan. Once you have this information, you can start laying the groundwork to conform to their requirements if you anticipate that you may want to borrow money in the future.

But be careful: Credit is nothing more than an agreement to pay *in the future*. It may be wise to *obtain* the credit now, but only incur obligations you can afford to pay based on your budget.

My friends will feel they have to take sides, and I'll end up losing them.

Divorce is one surefire way to weed out the "real" from the "fair weather" friends.

Good riddance to the friends who want to take sides based on money. And good riddance to the ones who feed off the spicy details they are getting from your spouse and not you.

It's a new beginning, and you're minus one spouse. It's as good a time as any to narrow down your friends to the ones you can really trust. Start being more discriminating. Don't be afraid. Think of it as a cleansing process.

Your true friends will stick by you. Years later you'll be able to laugh at what you shared during your divorce.

I won't have medical insurance.

In this day and age, medical insurance is a necessity of life. There are various ways to obtain medical insurance, and you need to determine which method suits your circumstances.

By way of a few examples, consider the following:

- You can obtain court orders requiring your spouse to continue maintaining you on medical insurance until your divorce is final.
- Your spouse can be ordered to maintain the children as beneficiaries of medical insurance.
- You may ask your spouse to agree voluntarily that part of your court order will require him or her to continue to pay for your insurance.
- You may want to obtain employment where medical insurance is one of the benefits.

Health Maintenance Organizations (HMOs) have very reasonably priced coverage, especially with high deductibles. You may be able to find national medical insurance companies that have plans for children only, with nominal monthly premiums. If those payments are still out of your price range, certain associations provide catastrophic medical insurance for real emergencies. These policies have very low premiums but very high deductibles.

Also, for non-emergency health care, hospitals in some major cities may have free clinics or clinics with sliding-scale fees based on income.

Talk to your accountant to see if you can deduct your medical insurance or your medical expenses. The law is continually changing in this area. Recent legislation includes medical savings account plans. Check it out.

If your spouse is employed by a company with more than twenty-five employees, you may be entitled to COBRA (Congressional Omnibus Budget Reconciliation Act) benefits. This would mean that you could remain on the insurance for three years at the same cost. Caveat: Beware of this "benefit," as you may find yourself unable to obtain affordable insurance at the end of the three years because at that time you may not qualify for insurance at favorable rates. Also, COBRA benefits may prove more costly than insurance you can purchase on your own.

Shop around for medical insurance. There are many different plans out there, and it may not be nearly as costly as you think.

Where will I get the money to pay for after-school activities, tutors, private school, or college for my children?

What you can "afford" is largely a function of how you allocate the money you have and how far you can make it stretch. Ideally, your settlement will provide for your former spouse to pay all or a portion of private school tuition, tutors, after-school activities, and college.

Be sure to raise all these issues with your attorney *before* you go to court or finalize any settlement. Remember, in a divorce, everyone has to make financial accommodations. Sometimes it is possible to work out compromises so that the status quo can be maintained for the children, although that often entails some sacrifices being made by you and your former spouse. For example, sales proceeds from an asset that would otherwise be divided by the parties can, by agreement, be set aside and earmarked for the payment of children's schooling, tutor, or other activities. Often a grandparent or family member would be happy to contribute to education expenses if they feel assured they will not be excluded from the child's life.

See if scholarships are available for school. Many after-school activities also make provisions for financial assistance. Sometimes, if you can volunteer, the fee for certain classes or activities will be discounted or waived.

Don't despair. Instead, be creative and flexible. If you and your former spouse both want your children's education to be a priority, there are ways to accomplish that goal.

I'll be denied custody of my children if I'm dating.

Absolutely not true.

Contrary to what some people believe, there is life during and after divorce. And you're allowed to live it. But use common sense!

Although the laws of each state vary, the essential elements that the courts consider do not. All judges want to know what is in the best interests of children and how each parent meets those needs.

No one considers social isolation a necessity or even a virtue. A stable relationship may even increase your chances of obtaining custody. Dating is perfectly fine and should not impact your chances of obtaining custody—unless you are behaving inappropriately. Most of us know what inappropriate is, but in case you're feeling too stressed to think it through clearly, here is a list of definite "don'ts":

- Don't leave your children alone when you go out. Be sure to have a responsible person watching the kids at all times.
- Don't stay out all night when the children are in your custody.
- Don't drink excessively with your date (or ever) in front of your children.
- Don't engage in sexual behavior in a location where your children could pay a surprise visit.
- Don't neglect your children because you are so busy courting, sparking, and trying to impress your significant other.

- Don't obtain a reputation for trolling singles bars.
- Don't miss important events in your children's lives.
- Don't miss your children's doctor's appointments or parent/teacher conferences because you are too busy with your new paramour.

It is your responsibility to make sure that dating does not put your children at risk in any way. Be a responsible parent first, and then have a good time!

I will have to get a job.

And if that's the case, you may as well get a new attitude. Consider it an adventure, a new beginning.

For those of you who have never worked outside the home, the terror of thinking about a job will probably be far worse than actually working.

For those of you who worked, hated it, and hoped never to work again, look for something you like better than the job you had before.

If you haven't worked in years and your skills are rusty or nonexistent, you may benefit from refresher courses or career courses at local colleges or high schools. Before you make job applications and have to appear at job interviews, consider whether you should first attend these courses.

If you have young children, it is emotionally and physically challenging to work outside the home. Make sure you know the availability, cost, and hours of child care before you commit to a job. You must be sure you'll be earning more than it costs to pay for child care while you work.

Working is a little like jumping into a cold swimming pool—there's an initial shock to your system, and then you get used to the water.

I'll have no time for myself, between working full-time and being a full-time parent.

You're right. But find the time anyway. Otherwise, the demands of working full-time and being a full-time parent will overwhelm you. Then, you won't be able to cope at home or at work.

Everyone needs some time; find those cracks for yourself. Approach the problem optimistically and creatively. Learn to budget your time the way you budget your finances. Look for activities that don't take a lot of time but will make you feel better—reading, listening to music, playing darts, gardening, playing pick-up games of basketball, playing chess, and so on.

Get your children on a homework schedule so they know what time has been set aside to help them with school problems. Carpool. Network with other parents—you're not the only one who needs a break. Let your children know that while you care for them and are available to help them during specified hours, you also need some adult time and your own quiet time. Go out with friends and on dates. No child was ever neglected because she spent an evening with a babysitter.

I'll be fired when:

- My employer finds out that my spouse has subpoenaed all of my work records.
- I take time away from my job to work on my case.

Involvement in litigation is not a good or valid reason for termination. Nonetheless, the fear of losing your job has some basis. Many employers are allowed to fire you without cause. If you anticipate losing time from work or expect that your employer will be required to appear in court, produce records, or be deposed, it's a good idea to give your employer as much advance notice as possible.

Schedule a short meeting to explain what is going on. Try to coordinate a work schedule to make up the time you will have to miss. Talk to your attorney about methods of getting work records to the other side in a manner that will cause your employer the least amount of hardship or none at all.

It's especially important to maintain your work performance. At a time when your employer is going to be inconvenienced by your litigation, don't give your employer a good excuse for finding fault with you.

Your employer won't fire you because records are subpoenaed. You may be fired or demoted, however, if you miss an excessive amount of time from work or the quality of your work suffers because you can't concentrate or don't have time to do a good job. This is true for any employee who is not fulfilling his or her job duties.

This is one of those times when you need to take control of your situation rather than letting it control you.

We'll end up in bankruptcy.

Unfortunately, this is an area over which you may have little control. It is usually advisable to avoid bankruptcy if at all possible. But if your spouse files, you may have no choice but to file as well. If the order dividing your assets is not final and you are still married to your spouse who files bankruptcy, your assets may be thrown into the bankruptcy. This is frustrating, inconvenient, and can be costly.

The good news is that divorce does not have to lead to bankruptcy. If money is tight and there are numerous bills to be paid, you and your spouse should consider opting for the lesser of two evils. In other words, work together instead of driving yourselves into bankruptcy court.

Mediation of your divorce may be a better option than litigation. With few assets, financial problems, and no money to litigate, your goals for settlement may be closer than you imagine.

Some parties use bankruptcy or the threat of bankruptcy to gain an advantage in the divorce. Some parties make the threat solely to intimidate. However, bankruptcy does not discharge child or spousal support (alimony) orders, and the "automatic stay" in bankruptcy is not available as a shield for a party who does not want to pay ordered support. Further, payments to equalize the division of property may not be dischargable in bankruptcy. This change in the law has knocked the wind out of the sails of the "bankruptcy threat."

This is an area where compromise may benefit both of you.

Will I have to give up therapy because of money considerations? What do I do about uninsured medical and dental expenses?

Again, this is an area where it's important that you talk to your attorney *before* you go to court or enter into a settlement. The responsibility for these obligations can and should be covered in your court orders.

Typically, payment of children's medical insurance will rest with the spouse who had coverage through a plan at his or her place of employment. Responsibility for the children's insurance premiums may be allocated between the parties or assigned to one party. The same is true for the uninsured and unreimbursed expenses the children incur.

Particularly if you are not the parent who generally takes the children to the doctor, it is important to provide that neither parent has the right to run up large bills for the children for which there is no coverage, except in cases of emergency. The consequence of incurring unauthorized medical bills is full payment by the parent who did not obtain approval for such treatment. This is especially true with psychiatric and psychological care, which often are excluded from insurance coverage. If you anticipate that your children may need this type of care, it's smart to get the parameters for payment built into your settlement or judgment.

Investigate whether there are free or discount treatment programs maintained by local hospitals or large universities. You'll have to decide what priority to give this budget item if your funds are limited. Before commencing any program for long-term treatment, get an evaluation of how long the treatment will be necessary in order to determine if you can afford the expense. If you or your child has a serious diagnosed psychological or psychiatric illness, there are federal and state programs available to assist you.

Don't be afraid to ask questions, and never hesitate to make inquiries about programs or methods that may save you money.

How will I ever see my children if my spouse moves with them out of the state or hundreds of miles away?

Judges want what is best for children, and no one can dispute that frequent and continuing contact with both parents is of paramount importance to a child's well-being.

Though the frequency and the contact may be reduced, your relationship and time with your children will not end if your spouse moves. Assuming a decision has been made, whether by agreement or court order, that your former spouse and children may move a significant distance away, it is critical that your court order include some schedule for long and frequent periods of visitation as well as telephone contact with your children. Don't leave this to be worked out later. Although it can always be modified or supplemented, it is still necessary to include a schedule that, at the very least, provides for visitation with the children for a portion of time or alternating such holidays as Christmas vacation, spring break, Thanksgiving, and long weekends if distance permits. In addition, the children should spend some portion of the summer with you.

The court order should spell out who pays for the children's travel as well as who will accompany them.

The less you leave to chance, the better the odds are that you will be able to see your children often in spite of the move.

Birthdays, communion, bar or bas mitzvah, graduation—are my children going to miss out on those special events because I can't afford the expense?

Your children won't necessarily miss out, but the celebration may have to be done differently.

If you and your former spouse can pool funds or work together to make special occasions as enjoyable for your children as they were before the divorce, go to the head of the class! You both have earned an A+ in co-parenting. But don't be disappointed if that's not the case. It rarely is.

Celebrations for special events may have to be significantly scaled down to your new economic conditions. Your children will understand. This is a chance to test your creativity. You can have a theme graduation party at your home just as easily as a fancy reception at an expensive restaurant. Kids enjoy pizza as much as a catered dinner. Don't think you're alone when it comes to budget constraints. What about calling other parents to see if they would like to combine celebrations to cut down on expenses. The list is endless.

I'll end up living on the street.

No, you won't.

Face it: After a divorce, each party ends up with roughly one-half of what they had during marriage. This is an adjustment you are forced to make. Everyone has some marketable skills. If you are objective about your real needs and set realistic goals, you can make it financially. Coupled with determination and desire, you have a winning combination.

The legal system, even with its imperfections, protects most of us. The system is *designed* to balance the needs of the parties and their children. Child support and spousal support, more commonly known as alimony, should alleviate some of the financial pressures associated with the necessities of life. The paying spouse should recognize that there are built-in limitations on how much can be demanded. There are agencies where one can apply for financial assistance. Shelters are available to house battered spouses and their children.

And, of course, there is your major resource: yourself.

No one will want to marry someone who has children.

Surprise: There are many people who would jump at the chance for a ready-made family. Lots of men and women out there love children and will love *your* children because they love you. You and the kids are a package deal. While some people will not date divorcees with children, others are eager to join a family environment and would be happy to accept financial as well as quasi-parental responsibility.

Our society is now filled with blended families. You are not alone, nor are you undesirable. When one client's husband left after she prosecuted him for assault, he arrogantly told her that nobody would marry a woman with four children, ages eighteen months to fourteen years. Eight months later she was happily married to a man who loved her and her children. Their wedding took place on his spacious estate.

If you find yourself falling for a non-family type, perhaps it's time to look at that person more carefully and move on.

The litigation will never end.

Yes, it will. It only *seems* like forever.

And you have more control than you think. If things are moving too slowly or it looks as if you and your spouse will never settle, tell your attorney that you want the case set for trial. If your attorney tells you that certain work must be accomplished before requesting a trial date, then sit down with your lawyer and find out what needs to be done, then do it. Set up a realistic schedule for getting it accomplished. Make sure you're kept in the loop on how things are progressing and whether the case is moving along as planned.

Like a book, there is a beginning, middle, and end. In busier jurisdictions a divorce can take a lot longer than you might expect. It's good to find out in advance approximately how long it takes to get a trial date in your court. Then you have a yardstick by which to measure your progress. If your jurisdiction takes nine months to set a trial date, there's no point getting upset if you're in month four and the case is still going on.

Don't be discouraged or frustrated by the numerous continuances that seem to plague litigation and the fact that the system moves slowly. Litigation is prolonged in some rare cases, because of appeals or really conflict-driven parties. As long as you remain on schedule, allow the divorce its gestation period. There will be closure.

2

THINGS TO DO BEFORE
IT STARTS

Get Ready

Gather copies of all financial and other important documents,
including tax returns, loan applications, wills, trusts, financial
statements, banking information, loan documents, credit card
and credit line statements, deeds to real property, car registration, insurance inventories, and life, medical, disability, and
auto insurance policies.

You may be scared, angry, depressed, or anxious. No matter what
you're feeling, if the process is starting, be armed and prepared.

Divorce is treated like a business. The court and the attorneys
will expect to review and rely on the records of financial transac-
tions during your marriage. Moreover, lawyers and the court will
use income tax returns and loan applications to track down income, assets, and debts that might otherwise be "overlooked" or
forgotten.

Your attorney needs all financial documents. The more you
can supply at the inception of your divorce, the easier and less
costly it will be. Try to discreetly gather and copy important documents. Don't forget about income records; retirement/pension
information; employer policies and benefits; records about
money lent to and borrowed from others; copyrights; royalties;

and information about proprietorships, partnerships, professional corporations, and family-owned businesses. If you have a document reflecting the ownership of any interest in an asset or any kind of debt, copy it and put the original in a safe place. *Make sure you advise your attorney about all documents.*

Don't worry about the cost of photocopying. If you are in a situation in which you don't control the finances or information, *copy everything and anything* that looks even mildly interesting—and make sure you copy the entire document, not just the part you think has valuable information. While all this copying may be expensive, we can assure you that it's far less expensive than hiring your attorney or an investigator to discover this information through formal procedures.

Don't worry about invading your spouse's privacy. You're not. You have an equal right to all these documents. You should have had access to these documents throughout your marriage. If you didn't, you'll have access to them in your divorce!

In one case a client photocopied her husband's day sheets from his medical practice. We discovered his handwritten notations documenting cash received each day. When the same documents were produced in response to subpoenas, the penciled notations had vanished. The doctor had a lot of explaining to do.

If you feel your spouse may not be completely candid about income, and he or she keeps a calendar or other document with appointments or names of clients, customers, or patients, copy that as well.

Although gathering copies of all documents is extremely helpful, don't panic if you can't do it. Your lawyer should be able to obtain the same information through discovery. It is helpful if you can get the financial papers at the beginning, but not critical. Remember that even with the most secretive of spouses, the accountant who prepared your *joint* income tax return has an equal obligation to both of you. You can ask the accountant to provide you with a copy of your tax returns, and you're entitled to them.

Information is power. This is a truism in divorce. The more information you have, the better off you are.

Make a list of assets and debts with as much specificity as possible.

Detail names of financial institutions, their location, account numbers, account names, and balances. Inventory safe deposit boxes with a witness. Record all information regarding any money you and your spouse owe to anyone and any money owing to you or your spouse, including loans, security deposits, and utility deposits.

It is much easier to sit down and put together this type of list before IT starts. Start compiling this information before the process begins and your spouse has an opportunity to make things "disappear." Trust us. Information and documentary evidence can "vanish."

One woman told her spouse their marriage was over *before* she filed, *before* she had restraining orders, and *before* she gathered together documents. The next day she found the filing cabinet containing all their financial records completely cleaned out. Subpoenas and accountants' records helped recreate most of the documents, but the notes, receipts, personally prepared financial statements, and handwritten notations could never be replaced.

If you have photocopied or written down account numbers, names, dollar amounts, and addresses, your lawyer will have a starting point for questions and subpoenas should your spouse choose not to act ethically.

Even if your spouse is completely aboveboard and will produce everything, it is helpful for your attorney to have as much information as possible at the start of your case. It gives your lawyer some idea about what you may expect, how to proceed, what may be realistic to request, and what a fair settlement might be.

Before things start, while your mind is still clear, write down as specifically as possible and in the most organized way everything you know about your financial situation. You are in a far better position to have access to information and to get questions answered before you and your spouse are adversaries. Write down everything you learn that may be relevant in the divorce. If you're not sure, write it down anyway.

It's helpful to make lists of assets and "related debts," such as the value of your house with the mortgage owed and the value of your car and the amount still owing. If you have documents confirming that information, even better. Don't leave out debts or other obligations, such as lawsuits or installment payments. Get information about the value of your house from local realtors before the divorce commences. A realtor can provide you with a practical, expense-free, and efficient way to make that information available to your attorney. (Just be careful, however, that the person you contact understands your need for privacy.) You can get a copy of the deed and a copy of the mortgage statement showing the monthly payment and the balance owed.

Don't throw your hands up in the air and say you can't do it. Like any homework assignment, the worst part is getting started.

There's no need to get caught up in guilt. You're not being tricky or devious. You are entitled to this information.

Write down names, telephone numbers, and addresses of anyone who may have useful information or who is a potential witness.

It will make life easier for your attorney and ultimately for you. It's a good idea to sit down and thoughtfully compile this type of list as soon as possible. Include in your list accountants, spouse's employer and coworkers, children's teachers and doctors, stockbrokers, realtors, bankers, housekeepers, neighbors, and friends.

Before your mind is bombarded with the tribulations of litigation, write down names of possible witnesses and include notes about what they may be qualified to testify about and what they might have witnessed. At the same time, it is helpful to make a list of possible adverse witnesses and people who you anticipate will be witnesses for your spouse. Include a short explanation as to why certain people may be witnesses against you.

For your own reference and file, keep a copy of all the information you give your attorney.

Depending on the issues in your case, some of these names may be the starting point for discussions with your attorney. The names on your list may trigger questions for your attorney and answers from you that lead your case in an unexpected direction. The list will make it easier for your attorney to telephone and interview people, and issue subpoenas if necessary.

Accumulate a cash account for hiring an attorney.

Attorneys don't work for free, and the one you hire is going to want a retainer, an "up-front" payment to secure his or her services. The retainer can vary from $100 to $25,000 depending on many factors, including the issues involved and their complexity, the size of the estate, and where you live.

So if you've decided to end the marriage and you're not the spouse with access to funds, it would be prudent to start setting aside a "stash" as soon as possible. You'll need those funds to retain a lawyer when you are ready to begin.

If you don't want your spouse to know you have consulted an

attorney, don't write a check. Pay in cash, have someone else write the check, or obtain a money order or bank check.

You may find a lawyer who will wait to be paid after the case has been filed, but don't count on it. Avoid placing yourself in a position where you are forced to hire someone who is not your preference, but will represent you without a retainer. Plan ahead. If you do not have money available, you may need several months or longer to accumulate enough money to pay for a consultation or retainer. Set aside money from whatever source you can and as often as you can so that you will have sufficient funds to hire the attorney of your choice.

Friends and family may be willing to lend you funds. Borrowing against a credit line or credit card is not the best solution, but sometimes it's the only one. Be creative but keep it legal.

Even if you are not ready to start, consult an attorney as soon as possible. Get referrals to two or more knowledgeable family law attorneys.

You may be on the fence about your marriage. If that's the case, it's better to err on the side of caution and get some legal advice before you jump off the fence. You don't just need advice, however, you need *good* advice.

Lawyers know how to make people like them, so don't be surprised if you find that you trust and admire the first lawyer you meet. But that may not be the best reason to hire him or her.

Who your attorney is will play a big part in the outcome of your divorce. Take a long look at the factors that count:

- your attorney's experience level;
- how smart and well acquainted your attorney is with family law;
- how well you get along with your attorney;

- whether your attorney will pay attention to you and to your case;
- how well your attorney works with your spouse's attorney.

Get the names of a few competent lawyers. Interview and shop around a little. It's always good to have some basis for comparison. Unlike other things you regularly shop for, this item is completely new to you. Be wise. This is a major purchase.

Remember, if you're thinking about divorce, your spouse may well be thinking along the same lines. You will be one step ahead if you have already done your homework by having selected an attorney. This way you're covered when you decide to proceed or if your spouse surprises you and files first!

There are many places to get referrals. Word of mouth and recommendations from people you know and trust are always good sources. You can contact state and local bar associations. Therapists, counselors, doctors, accountants, ministers, and rabbis are also often knowledgeable about attorneys who have been helpful to others in your situation.

Even if you are not ready to file, it's a good idea to consult an attorney to get some input as to what you should be doing and what you should avoid. Just because you are armed with the knowledge that you will be ending the marriage soon doesn't mean you're savvy about all the ins and outs and do's and don'ts. Get some informed advice in advance. You can never be too prepared.

Remove to a safe place outside your home valuables that can be taken or broken, potentially dangerous items, and objects of sentimental significance.

What are we talking about? Easy. Things such as jewelry, guns, mementos, letters, and keepsakes of value.

If there are weapons in your home, remove them to a safe place outside your home. Divorces frequently get worse before they get better. Why should either of you succumb to an irrational temptation to do harm to the other or another family member in a moment of rage? Remove anything that can become dangerous during an impulsive moment. Some attorneys are willing to safeguard these items, or you can put them in storage or in a safe deposit box if they fit.

Every spouse knows the things that are meaningful to the other. Often they may be things of value, such as jewelry, but sometimes it's something nostalgic or sentimental: a photograph, a letter, a book from a special friend, a trophy. Remove these items from your home and put them somewhere for safekeeping. But be reasonable. The Sony television is replaceable. The letter from Aunt Emily before she died is one of a kind. Secure special things somewhere safe from your spouse's wrath. If you say your spouse "isn't like that," we hope you're right. But why take the chance?

Videotape, photograph, or inventory house contents and make copies of any existing lists of contents.

When a divorce starts, it's amazing how things can disappear. Then how do you prove it was there in the first place? Pictures provide evidence of ownership, condition and worth. Videotape, photograph, or at the very least inventory the contents of your home. There's no downside and only an upside. Pictures speak louder than words.

While you may believe you can remember every detail of your home, those memories will fade quickly if you're not living there, and you may forget items "removed" by your spouse. Therefore, before anything is said about divorce, try to videotape your entire house and its contents and furnishings, including personal effects such as jewelry, sports equipment, and tools. At the very least, make sure you have a list of the contents of your house, especially anything valuable. Write down the name of the manufacturer and the pattern of expensive items such as silver, crystal, or china. For art, antiques, or collections, make note of all identifying information. If you already have a list of your possessions for insurance purposes, copy that list and put it someplace safe.

Cancel credit cards, get new ones issued in your own name, and set up bank accounts in your name alone.

This is easy and important. Don't be lazy about it. Do it and save yourself a lot of grief as well as some accounting expenses down the road. Don't do it, and you may find yourself with financial headaches that will leave you reeling.

Cancel all joint credit cards. Any charges your spouse puts on those cards after you separate may be his or her responsibility according to the divorce court but *not* according to your creditor. American Express is not really interested in your marital soap opera. All they know is that both names appear on the card, and if it's not paid, they're going to sue *both* of you. If they can't collect from your spouse, they will have no problem garnishing your wages or levying on your bank accounts even though the charges were not made by you.

It is not uncommon for spouses shortly before and during a divorce to run up a large credit card debt. Let your spouse do it on a card in his or her name alone. As hard as it is to imagine, you can end up with your credit destroyed simply because your spouse was irresponsible and all you did was cosign on the card.

Get credit cards in your own name. You can start building your own credit if you don't already have it, and you will also protect yourself from your spouse's actions. By getting new credit cards issued in your own name you prevent your spouse from using credit in your name for which you may be liable. You also prevent your spouse from leaving you with no credit, which happens when your name is removed from all credit cards or all jointly held credit cards are canceled.

Open bank accounts in your name alone so that you can operate independently of your spouse and without the necessity of sharing information or getting agreements for withdrawals. There may be expenses, such as security deposits or attorneys' fees, about which you do not want to alert your spouse. If you have your own account, you have a measure of privacy. Do not forget, however, that all your account information can be reviewed by your spouse if formally requested.

Take your children to a therapist if you anticipate custody problems.

The goal is to have a peaceful divorce, particularly with respect to issues involving your children. But goals can be like good intentions. Some people know in advance that there will be a problem concerning custody. If you are one of those parents, don't bury your head in the sand. Under those circumstances it may prove wise to take your children to a counselor to speak about their feelings and any problems they are having with your spouse.

If you believe that custody will be litigated, you may wish to have your children evaluated by a therapist before your spouse tries to influence the children. Don't ignore the possibility that your children may discuss this appointment with your spouse, and be prepared for any possible ramifications. You should also seek advice concerning your children's need for help in coping with the stress of divorce.

A declaration or testimony will be needed from a mental health professional if you are going to ask for unusual or restrictive court orders concerning your spouse's custodial time with the children. It can be helpful to your case if your children have seen a therapist before you start the process. This individual can give a neutral explanation to the court why the request you are making is in your children's best interests.

A judge may not believe your stories, but it's astounding the impact those same stories have on the court when related by an independent mental health professional who has no ax to grind. A client went to court, representing herself, to obtain monitored visitation. She alleged that her husband was physically abusing their children. The court not only denied her request but admonished her for requesting the relief. Three weeks later, when the wife's counsel submitted the declaration of the children's psychologist, the court immediately ordered monitored visitation, requiring another adult to be present when the husband saw the children, and awarded attorneys' fees to the wife.

Since many attorneys know mental health professionals who specialize in custody disputes, it's a good idea to consult with an attorney to get recommendations before you start the process. Whenever the case starts you will have a mental health professional lined up to testify. It is crucial to have someone who is familiar with the court process and knows what information the judge would like to hear.

As cold and calculating as this may sound, make no mistake: Nothing in family law is worse than a nasty custody battle. It is naive not to get all of your ducks in line before a battle begins.

Prepare your parents and children for what is going to occur; if possible, you and your spouse should agree on a plan for breaking the news to your children.

This is going to be hard, particularly if you maintained the facade of normalcy. Think about the best way and time to break the news.

A teacher kindly consoled a sixth grader, "I'm so sorry your parents are getting divorced." The child burst into tears because he was the last to know.

If both you and your spouse know the divorce is coming, by all means sit down together and work out how you are going to tell your children. They should not hear about it first from friends or neighbors. Try to practice the words. You will be nervous and upset, but, most important, you will need to reassure your children that both of their parents still love them. Avoid any explanation that places blame or fault on either of you or on the children. While it might feel good to point a finger and say the divorce has been caused by your spouse's infidelity, the person with whom you share that thought *should not be* your child. If you and your spouse have worked out a visitation or custody plan, share it with the children. They will be happier if they know their parents are united in plans for them. But the sharing stops there. Do not discuss the details of your financial arrangements with your children. This is only a burden to them, one to which they should not be subjected.

While you might think it's your children who will be the most seriously traumatized, ironically it may be *your parents* who fall apart at the news of your pending divorce. It's a good idea to coordinate with your parents to present a unified front to your children.

Although it is your divorce, family members and children will be caught up in the tidal wave. They need to be prepared for the changes that will be occurring and how those changes affect you and impact them.

Determine whose side housekeepers, sitters, teachers, and other individuals will take if a custody dispute arises.

Don't kid yourself. Everyone has an opinion, and everyone takes sides.

If you have the slightest concern that your case will evolve into a custody dispute, it's a good idea to talk to those who have close contact with your children. If you're discreet, you can find out whose side potential witnesses will take. See what they think of you and your spouse as parents and what signs they may have picked up from your children about their feelings toward you and your spouse. Find out if your children have voiced any complaints. Whether the feedback is positive or negative, having this information gives you an advantage and some valuable insight.

The kind of people who usually observe children and hear their praise and complaints are pediatricians, teachers, sitters, housekeepers, and other children's parents. You'd be surprised at the kind of remarks children make. For example, "My mom always helps me with my homework" or "My mom yells at me a lot" or "My dad plays ball with me every night" or "My dad is never home to spend time with me."

Talk to people. Find out what your children have said, how they act and how they feel. Sometimes outsiders pick up clues from children that are missed by parents. Sometimes children find it easier to confide in someone other than family. You are starting a potential witness list. Write down what people tell you and try to get them to be as specific as possible about what they heard, what they observed, and when it took place. All of this should be brought to your attorney's attention as soon as possible. Lawyers frequently want to get declarations from people while the memory is fresh. It is better to obtain declarations before these witnesses have had time to reflect on how they would "prefer not to be involved" and "don't really remember that well" anymore.

You may be disillusioned, but don't be surprised if some people testify in their own economic advantage. This is to be expected.

Try to make discreet inquiries before you disclose any information at all. If you feel the person is not in your camp, avoid any disclosures that might hurt you later. An employee who is financially dependent on you may turn out to be a "spy." However, if you fire that person and keep your privacy, you risk revenge. Over the years we have advised our clients not to retain housekeepers who continue to remain in the employ of their spouse. At best they are always in the middle. At worst you may be harboring a traitor and a spy in your house.

Don't sign anything presented to you by your spouse, but do try to get your spouse to sign a listing agreement if it is your desire to sell your house.

You may have signed everything placed before you when you were married. But now that the partnership is ending, don't act in the same spirit of trust. It may take some creativity to get out of automatically signing whatever is placed in front of you. Instead of signing the document, say you want to think about it, you want to talk to the accountant, you have to make dinner, you have to mow the lawn, you'll look at it tomorrow—and the list goes on. Then read, review, photocopy, and bring it to a lawyer first. These are the new rules and regulations by which you *must* live.

It's not a question of how smart you are. You will have no idea how favorably or unfavorably something signed will impact you in your divorce. Short of signing your child's report card, it is essential that you first show your attorney any document your spouse asks you to sign.

On the other hand, if you really want to sell your home and suspect your spouse will object once the divorce starts, get your spouse to sign a listing agreement before there is any suspicion of divorce. Once the real estate papers are signed and delivered, there can be little doubt that you both wanted the house sold. The court will probably enforce your agreement and make your spouse follow through with the sale, voluntarily or involuntarily.

Of course, a spouse who has read this book will know better than to sign. Hey, you lose nothing by trying!

Consider withdrawing at least one-half of the funds in joint bank accounts.

It's a joint account. It's yours, so take it if you need it. You may need the money to retain an attorney. You may need it for living expenses. If you might be in a position where either of these will be a problem without that money, you have little choice but to take it. There is the possibility that your spouse may take it all.

Some attorneys advise their clients to take it all and sort out restitution, if appropriate, later. We don't endorse that plan unless there are extreme circumstances. Cleaning out a bank account will not necessarily endear you to a judge or promote settlement with your spouse.

If you have ready access to enough money without touching the joint account, that may be preferable. But don't be a sucker. If virtually all your money is in joint accounts, don't wait to discover that your spouse was not nearly as considerate as you and the accounts have already been emptied, leaving you nothing.

If the divorce is your choice or if divorce is on the horizon, consider completing medical and dental work.

Once you separate, your spouse may not be obligated to pay for medical and dental expenses, and in most states your marital estate will not be required to pay for those expenses either.

There can be financial, emotional, and physical advantages to completing contemplated medical and dental work before separation. Here are some things to consider:

- With few exceptions, it is better not to be immersed in divorce when you are undergoing any medical or dental work that will leave you physically uncomfortable, tired, or debilitated. You should be at your strongest when embarking on divorce.

- If you are undergoing tests and evaluations for medical problems, you will naturally be distracted and need to give those procedures your full attention. The tests you are undergoing and the news you receive could be enough of an emotional drain. That's not the best time to jump into another and different emotional ordeal.

- Some medical and dental treatment is optional—such as cosmetic surgery—and may not be covered by insurance. Accordingly, you may be better served by having this work done while you are still an unseparated couple and paying this expense from joint savings or earnings. This type of treatment may be your sole financial responsibility after the divorce starts.

- Another consideration is the treatment you need and the duration of such care. If your medical and dental insurance is through your spouse's employer, find out in advance what coverage options will be available to you once you have separated and when the divorce is final. This answer may give you insight on the advisability of proceeding with medical and dental care before you start the divorce.

- If you find out that you have serious medical problems, that information may influence whether you initiate divorce.

Take the necessary steps to make or revise your will and any trusts.

Do you want to hear something dreadful? In most states if you die without a will, the bulk of your assets go to your spouse even if you're in the middle of a divorce. Oops!

Do not assume your will and trusts change because you've filed for divorce. They don't. If you have an existing will, revise it before you start the process. If you don't make changes, a court may require you to fulfill certain estate planning decisions made during happier times. If the lawyer who drafted your wills or trusts is the lawyer for you and your spouse, find another lawyer to make the changes, revisions, or redraft the documents the way you want them. If you don't have a will, it's a good idea to get one drawn up. Explain to the attorney that divorce is imminent and you want your share of the assets to go to beneficiaries you choose. If you have an existing trust, it's a good idea to consult with an attorney to see if any changes should be made. A family trust may require the consent and signature of your spouse. If that is the case, be sure to ask the attorney whether it would be wise to terminate or modify the trust when the divorce begins. Be sure to share this information with your divorce attorney so that he or she can coordinate with the estate planning lawyer to do what is best to protect you.

Don't let these "details" slip through the cracks. Take care of business *now*. When it comes to estate planning, there's no time like the present.

3

QUESTIONS TO ASK A PROSPECTIVE ATTORNEY— AND THINGS TO CONSIDER

Who Can I Turn To?

Is the attorney experienced in divorce law?

Ever heard the expression "Jack of all trades and master of none"? Some attorneys are convinced they are competent to do every type of law.

When interviewing an attorney for your divorce case, it is imperative to find out how much family law is practiced by the attorney. Sometimes lawyers want to increase their case load or, finding business slow, take on cases not in their area of expertise. The time to find this out is before—not after—you retain counsel.

It is not essential that you hire an attorney who practices *only* divorce work, but make sure his or her practice has a high percentage of family law cases. Let someone else be a lawyer's first divorce case, not you. In some cities there are lawyers who practice family law exclusively; in other places that may not be the case. To a great extent the complexity of your case will dictate how much family law experience your lawyer must have.

Don't be shy about asking questions. Don't be shy about probing. It is neither rude nor inappropriate. You are the watchdog of your future.

Is the attorney answering your questions?

Go to your first interview with an attorney armed with a battery of questions. It's okay if the attorney doesn't know "the" answer to a question. Not all questions have only one answer, and legal research and investigation may be required in order for the attorney to express an opinion. Your attorney can't and shouldn't predict the future, but he or she should still have a relatively good idea about what you can expect and what your options are. Vague but reassuring responses are not enough. Listen carefully to *how* the lawyer answers your questions. Has the lawyer been specific?

A client recently retained us after having met with another attorney who spent the entire interview discussing his retainer and fees, while never answering any questions posed by the client.

If you are getting platitudes and hand holding but very little concrete information, point this out to the lawyer and see if you can get more focused responses. If not, keep shopping for the right attorney.

Is your lawyer asking you questions to get some insight into your priorities and needs?

Only you know what is important to you. Your attorney is not a mind reader, and this is not a guessing game. Each case has its own personality; it's important to tune into whether your attorney is giving your case the personalized attention it requires or is just treating it like more inventory.

It's important to evaluate whether your attorney is asking you questions that will provide an insight into what you hope to accomplish, what your priorities are, and what you need and want for the future. As an example, if keeping your house is your number one priority, does your attorney know this? Have you discussed the likelihood of this happening, and has he or she strategized with you about how to accomplish this goal? The same would be true for any other priority you have, ranging from something as small as keeping the picture given to you and your spouse by your favorite deceased aunt to obtaining an order allowing you and your children to move three thousand miles away.

Although you have the ability to bring up subjects that are important to you when you meet with your attorney, only you can decide whether your lawyer is giving your priorities and needs the attention you believe they require. If not, assess whether you have prioritized correctly. Make sure your lawyer is "getting it." If that's not happening, perhaps you should be seeking other representation.

Is there a rapport between you and the lawyer? Can you and your lawyer work as a team?

Hiring an attorney for your divorce is very much like entering into a short-term marriage. Your attorney holds a lot of your future in his or her hands. Just as in marriage, this person should be someone you trust, someone you can easily question and confide in, someone with whom you feel comfortable. Try to make a better decision than you did with your spouse, or this relationship could also end up in "divorce."

A client should never be intimidated by his or her own attorney. It happens a lot, although some clients are too afraid to admit it.

On the flip side, your attorney should offer guidance based on experience. If you don't feel confident and you second-guess every single decision, your antennae should warn you there is danger.

Success is often built on chemistry. If you feel your attorney isn't interested in you, doesn't support you, or actively dislikes you, discuss your feelings with your attorney or, alternatively, terminate the relationship. Sometimes two people don't click.

One woman came to us in distress about the attorney currently representing her, a highly regarded attorney. When asked why she felt compelled to make a change, she responded, "The truth of the matter is, I'm more scared of my attorney than I ever was of my husband."

You and your attorney are working together. You're on the same team, and more can be accomplished with team effort than with two players working at cross purposes.

Look before you leap! Investigate hourly rates, billing increments, and all billing procedures. Are you charged for staff time, and, if so, at what rate?

It's terrible to find yourself arguing about money with your own attorney, especially when that person is supposed to be protecting your financial interests. Who you select will, to some degree, be dictated by finances. Get the monetary issues straight from the start to avoid confusion later.

Don't get into the mind-set that you don't like to talk about money. You *have* to talk about money. Ask the right questions when you interview an attorney and you may never have to cross that bridge again. So for starters, be sure to do the following:

Ask the attorney about his or her hourly rate; find out if that rate will stay the same during the entire case. Compare attorneys' hourly rates to see what is standard in your area. Remember, divorce lawyers' rates in the same area may vary greatly depending on the experience and reputation of the attorney as well as the complexity of the cases he or she is accustomed to handling.

Although some people shop for the lowest hourly rate, this can be a costly mistake. What your attorney accomplishes in the time billed is what is really important. If it takes an experienced attorney one hour to draft a document and the attorney's hourly rate is $300, your bill is $300. If it takes a less experienced attorney two hours to draft the same document and that attorney's hourly rate is $200, your bill is $400. Moreover, if you hire an inexperienced attorney who makes mistakes, it will be expensive to hire another attorney to try to rectify those mistakes. Be mindful. Some "mistakes" can't be fixed.

Find out about increments of billing. Some attorneys bill in minimum increments of quarter hours, others in tenths of hours. What this means is that *the least you are billed* for any work on your case is either fifteen minutes if quarterly increments or six minutes if the billing is in tenths of hours. Attorneys are not usually willing to negotiate the increments because their entire billing system is based on these increments. The time increments can often impact your bill significantly. If the billing increments are quarter hours, ask what the attorney does about billing for a five-minute phone call. Don't assume that the fee package quoted by the first attorney you interview necessarily reflects what other lawyers in your area are charging.

Double billing can increase your bill geometrically, so you really need to understand it and, if possible, negotiate your fee agreement to avoid it, except when specifically authorized by you. Double billing means that you are billed for each attorney when two attorneys in the firm confer about your case. If you are being double billed, the rate you are charged for one hour is the sum of both lawyers' hourly rates. This is a matter to discuss *before* you sign the retainer agreement. If you have objections to the agreement and can't work them out, go elsewhere. *Whatever verbal agreement you reach about billing should be set forth clearly in the retainer agreement.*

There are usually other individuals working in the lawyers' office besides attorneys. Are you billed for the time of these individuals, and if so, at what rate? The support staff can include secretaries, legal assistants, paralegals, and law clerks. Recognize that these extra expenses can add up and must be factored in when you are deciding if you can afford this firm.

Most attorneys bill for paralegal time. Some attorneys bill for secretarial time, including setting up your file. Some charges border on overreaching. Frankly, if an attorney insists on charging you for secretarial time, you should seriously consider if this is the firm for you.

Before you sign on the dotted line, make sure you know exactly the services for which you are agreeing to be billed and the rate each person charges.

Be sure to inquire about the expertise of associates, what is delegated to them, and the rates charged by them.

If your case ends up in court, you will hardly be in the mood for surprises. Unfortunately, many clients have had the experience of hiring an attorney to handle all aspects of their case, only to find it has been delegated to an unknown associate. Going to court can be a rattling experience, and meeting your attorney for the first time, minutes before the hearing, can be even more unnerving. There is no need to have these types of surprises. When you interview attorneys, ask questions to eliminate surprises. Some things you'll want to know:

Does the law firm have associates, and if so, will the associates be working on your case? "Associates" are usually lawyers in the firm who are not partners. Their title is not important. What is important is the amount of experience they have and what aspect of your case they will be assigned. What are their hourly rates? What work is delegated to them? Will the attorney or the associate be answering your questions, conducting discovery, taking depositions, conferring with opposing counsel, making the court appearances, preparing the paperwork in your case? If the answer to enough of these questions is "the associate," you should be meeting this individual as well as the attorney you are hiring.

It is also appropriate to ask about the associate's experience. How long has he or she been practicing law with the firm, and how much of the practice has been in family law? To what extent does the partner supervise the associate's work and billing? The billing rate of associates is lower than that of a partner, so having an associate do research or legwork can save you money if the right tasks are delegated and properly supervised.

If you want only a particular attorney, such as a specific partner or the head of the firm, to represent you in court or do other assignments, before signing the retainer agreement you must discuss this point, find out if it's possible, negotiate that provision, and make sure the provision appears in your retainer agreement.

While in the throes of the emotional trauma of the breakup, it is difficult to select an attorney and negotiate a retainer contract. Do the best you can. This advice is intended to keep you out of a divorce battle with your attorney while you are divorcing your spouse.

Familiarize yourself with the procedures your attorney uses for hiring experts.

In many divorce cases, experts must be hired; for example, there are forensic accountants, psychiatrists, real estate appraisers, and actuaries. Your attorney should select experts known to be competent and well suited for your kind of case. Your retainer agreement should contain specific provisions regarding your attorney's authority to hire these experts. Is an expert absolutely necessary in your case? Does the attorney consult with you and obtain your consent before retaining the expert? Does the expert require a retainer? Will he or she be paid from the retainer you gave your attorney? Will you need to come up with additional money for the expert? What happens when the expert has used up the retainer? What if you cannot come up with more funds? Be sure to inquire if additional fees are required if your expert must testify in court.

You should have a written retainer agreement with any expert that contains at least the following:

1. Exact nature of services to be performed.
2. Fees charged, including the rate for each person whose fees may be billed to you.
3. The amount of the retainer and whether it is refundable.

Will you receive copies of all correspondence and pleadings?

A feeling you don't want to experience in your divorce case is that you are being left out of the loop. Most clients want to know everything that is happening, and they absolutely should know everything. There is no reason that clients shouldn't have their own file that is virtually identical to their attorney's file. This means you should have a copy of every piece of paper of any kind that goes out of or into your lawyer's office.

It will cost you more money—at the very least for the copies and perhaps also for attorneys' fees for the cover letter—but being apprised of all that is happening is worth the extra expense. Be sure to read and consider what you've received. If you don't, you're just wasting money and may be missing crucial information.

Make sure it is the policy of the lawyer's office to send you a copy of *everything*. If for any reason that is not the standard operating procedure, request that it be changed for you. If it cannot, consider if you can be happy with an arrangement that leaves you in the dark. Probably not.

Do you participate in meetings with attorney and experts?

Discuss with your attorney which meetings with experts you will attend. Participating in meetings is a good way to gauge the progress of your case, give input, if necessary, and trigger new ideas and directions. It also enables you to monitor how your lawyer and expert are coordinating and strategizing.

The more they understand you and your case, the better job they can do for you. Many times, as a result of client participation, crucial facts and issues come up in these meetings.

Jump in and participate!

Retainer agreements should be in writing and contain all terms and all information of major importance to the client.

Always have a *written* retainer agreement with your attorney. In many states this is required by law. The advantages are numerous. At a minimum, the retainer agreement should contain the "deal points," spelling out exactly what matter is being handled and what the attorney's obligations are with respect to performance. It should also state what is expected from you financially. The agreement should indicate the rates for everyone for whom you will be charged as well as the increments in which you will be billed. It should also detail any other expenses for which you are billed, such as photocopying, postage, long-distance calls, filing fees, and so on. The retainer agreement should state how often you will receive billings. Once a month is most common. It should also state whether or not the billing is itemized. This is important. You *do* want your bills to have a breakdown detailing the time expended, the rate charged, the services performed by the attorney and each staff member, and an itemization of costs.

The retainer agreement must include the amount of the retainer you will be paying. Look to see if the agreement addresses certain possibilities: What happens if your case is concluded and the retainer is not used up in its entirety? What if you terminate the services of your attorney before using up the retainer? What if you and your spouse decide to reconcile and dismiss the case? Is the unused portion of your retainer refundable under these or any other circumstances? You may want that spelled out in the agreement.

If the retainer is nonrefundable, the amount paid becomes an important factor. Try to keep the nonrefundable retainer small to avoid losing a large sum in the event you and your attorney part company for any reason. Obviously, it is more advantageous if the unused portion of the retainer is refundable, and it is not unreasonable to make that request.

Another matter typically addressed in retainer agreements is how fee disputes between you and your own attorney will be handled. If this is included, be sure to read this section carefully and make sure it is fair to both you and the lawyer. If you are really uncertain, you can actually take the retainer agreement to another attorney to be reviewed. Although few people choose to do this, it is an option. In any event, before you sign the agreement, be sure you understand the financial commitment you are making.

Keep in mind that the retainer agreement should be a document you can easily understand. If it is not, have your attorney make changes until it is in a form you find understandable and easy to follow. Always keep a copy of the retainer agreement you have signed.

What happens when the attorney goes on vacation?

It's a good question, and you should ask your lawyer this when you do your interviewing. Your case continues even in your lawyer's absence. Although your lawyer has the right to take a vacation, it's important to know what kind of provisions have been made in case something important comes up in your attorney's absence.

If you're lucky, the entire office doesn't close, although sometimes that does happen. Usually, when attorneys go on vacation, they have another attorney who covers for them. In most instances, the covering attorney is a friend and someone who practices in a similar manner. Some attorneys close their office but leave a telephone number for emergency contacts while on vacation. Others leave strict orders that they will accept absolutely no client contact during their vacation.

Make sure your attorney advises you, your spouse's attorney, and the court before leaving on an extended vacation. If you have reason to believe there will be an emergency in your attorney's absence, make sure you know who will cover for your attorney, that the covering attorney is familiar with the facts and status of your case, and that you have his or her name, address, and telephone number. But remember that if you call and ask questions, you'll be billed as if you called your own lawyer.

What does the attorney consider the best approach to your case? Are you getting realistic, practical advice?

Okay, you're not a lawyer. But that doesn't mean you can't distinguish between someone who is providing realistic, practical advice and solutions and someone who is stroking you and telling you what you want to hear. Watch out for lawyers who are blowing smoke.

Certain things make no sense, and certain dreams are clearly pipe dreams. Don't look for someone who is feeding your fantasies. Look for someone who is telling it to you straight. If you would like your husband never to see your two children again but you know he has been an appropriate parent, be wary of an attorney who tells you that he'll fight to the end to prevent your husband from seeing the children. And if you've been married for thirty-five years to a woman who has always been a homemaker and you would like to pay no alimony at all, be wary of the attorney who's ready to fight that windmill.

It's not always easy to tell if you're getting good advice. Our advice is to ask a lot of questions and inquire about your attorney's strategy. Reflect on whether the advice really makes sense.

Frequently, there are several ways to approach a legal problem. In addition, there are levels of aggression appropriate to each case. It is of major importance for your attorney to have an approach or plan for your case that he or she can articulate. In order to move a case in a positive direction, there must be a well thought out plan and alternatives based on different scenarios. While the plan may change during the course of your case, if no plan is in place, your case is not being managed properly. If your attorney is only reacting when a crisis hits, change attorneys. Good lawyering involves action, not simply reaction. If your attorney is taking action only when you threaten to fire him or her, fire your attorney.

Your attorney should always consider (but not necessarily follow) approaches that you suggest. Your attorney should help you form reasonable expectations. If you have reasonable expectations, you can plan ahead with less anxiety.

In family law cases, common sense goes a long way. Make sure you understand your attorney's approach, that you generally understand the reasons for it, and that it makes sense. If it doesn't make good sense to you, it's possible it isn't realistic.

Will your case be filed in the most advantageous court? Does your attorney know the judge? Is he or she familiar with the rules and procedures of the court where your case will be heard?

All of these are important questions to ask the attorney you are interviewing. The answers may determine who you hire.

More often than not, there is only one court in which your case can be filed. Sometimes there is only one judge, and that is that. In some cases, however, a choice can be made about where to file your case because there is more than one court that handles divorce cases. If that is your situation, your attorney should discuss the advantages and disadvantages of filing in each place. Some courts have more time for lengthy hearings. Some courts have a reputation of ordering greater or lesser sums payable for support and fees. Some courts have different methods of approaching child custody cases. The attorney with whom you meet should know all of this and be able to advise you.

You should inquire as to whether or not your attorney has had cases before the judge who will be assigned to your case or, in larger jurisdictions where you may not yet know the assignment, how often your lawyer has appeared before the divorce judges. There is no reason for your attorney to be unfamiliar with the divorce judges where he or she practices. Naturally, you don't want to hire someone who is notorious for not getting along with the family law judiciary, so check this out.

Your lawyer should know the rules and procedures of the court where your case will be heard. You should not pay for the time spent learning about routine procedures. Also, when an attorney doesn't know the judges, the court, and the procedures, it's a lot easier to get "hometowned." This means that a judge and the court may feel more kindly toward opposing counsel, a familiar face.

I know you say it's supposed to be about justice, but the smart litigant gives justice a helping hand by making sure the case is filed in the most advantageous court and that the lawyer is experienced with this court, its rules, and the judge.

What is your lawyer's relationship with your spouse's attorney?

As strange as it may seem, the course of a case is frequently dictated by the relationship between opposing counsel. It's a good idea to ask a prospective attorney if he or she knows your spouse's lawyer. And if so, how do they work together?

When you're well into the case, it's a dismal discovery to learn that your lawyer and your spouse's lawyer do not get along, and a good portion of the fighting is the result of dueling egos rather than the particulars of your case. This can and does happen, though fortunately not too often. It's not essential that the lawyers like one another, but be sure you're not getting caught in the middle of a vendetta that has nothing to do with you.

If attorneys have had many cases opposing one another, you may find that they have very good feelings about each other. This can be advantageous. You won't have to pay them to dot every i and cross every t. It's not a problem if lawyers are cordial, even friendly, provided they are putting your case first. Don't think that because two attorneys get along or are friends, you will be sold out. Although that's possible, it isn't likely. Frequently, it will save you time and money if lawyers work well together and trust each other.

You're stuck with your spouse's choice of attorney, but you can still pick the best option for yourself.

How quickly will your calls be returned?

Watch out for lawyers who *never* return phone calls. The ones who call back a week or two or three later are only slightly better. And there are a lot of them out there.

Recognize that lawyers are busy, are frequently in court, and can't always get to a telephone every day. Unless you are a chronic caller or a complete pest (and that's one of the worst kind of clients to be), you should receive a return call within a reasonable period of time—about forty-eight hours or less. Circumstances can change that amount of time, but if your lawyer always takes a long time to call back, talk to him or her about it. During the initial interview, ask the attorney about his or her usual pattern with respect to returning phone calls. Although the lawyer is bound to say, "I'll call back promptly," ask what will be done if he or she is tied up in trial for many days. Will your calls be returned from the courthouse? Many lawyers do. Ask this question.

It's also a good idea to find out if there is a good person in the office—a partner, associate, paralegal, or secretary—you can speak with when your attorney is difficult to reach. Many routine inquiries can be fielded by someone other than your lawyer for no cost or a fraction of the cost. Consider this when you call in. Alternatively, you can write or fax your attorney to get answers to some questions.

If you feel your attorney is not communicating with you or is actually ducking your calls, schedule a conference immediately. If you don't even get a return call to schedule that conference, "let your fingers do the walking."

Which attorney will be appearing for you in court?

If there is more than one attorney in the office, ask this question when you interview lawyers. Sometimes attorneys send associates to court. Some hearings require experienced, sophisticated attorneys, and others don't. Find out who will appear for you at major hearings and decide whether you're comfortable with that attorney appearing for you. You have the right to know this in advance. You don't want to retain an attorney who thinks your case isn't big enough or important enough to take up his or her time. When that occurs, cases are often delegated to associates. It's a good idea to know in advance if you are going to get the person you hired.

Interview more than one attorney.
Keep interviewing until you feel you've made a connection. You don't marry the first person you date, and it's not necessarily a good idea to hire the first lawyer you interview. Even if you have extremely positive feelings, put hiring the individual on hold until you've had an opportunity to talk to at least one other lawyer and have some basis for comparison.

Interviewing a number of attorneys gives you an opportunity to see different points of view and different ways of approaching your case. It's always a good idea to have some grasp of your options.

This is your life. Try on a few attorneys and pick the one that fits you best.

Make sure your attorney has not represented your spouse or your spouse's business, or has any other conflict of interest.
It is the lawyer who should make sure there is no conflict of interest, but checks and balances have always been a wise and workable system. It never hurts for you to make sure that an attorney and your spouse's paths haven't crossed in a manner that poses a conflict of interest. If an attorney has a relationship with your spouse or your spouse's business, don't even consider that attorney. The smaller your community, the greater the possibility that a conflict may exist.

While watching their children play soccer, two men were chatting about their businesses and investments. One happened to be a family law attorney. The other was unhappily married. Imagine his dismay when the family law attorney to whom he had confided everything turned up as his wife's lawyer. The court had no trouble screaming "foul" and ordering the lawyer off the case.

In a nutshell, a conflict of interest can arise when an attorney has had any kind of contact with your spouse in which information that may be part of the divorce has been imparted. It does not necessarily have to arise from prior legal representation. If your spouse and the attorney met at a dinner party and talked at great length about, for example, the pros and cons of your spouse selling his business and what might be a fair price, that would be enough for a conflict of interest to exist. If your prospective attorney plays tennis with your spouse and they have talked about your children, think twice.

Your attorney should be your advocate only. You will be happier and better protected if you are dealing with an attorney who has not been involved in any dealings with your spouse.

4

PITFALLS

I Heard It Through the Grapevine

Don't be preoccupied with how your life "used to be."
Life goes on.

You can think about "the way it was" all you want, but that fixation will make you sad, crazy, or angry. So why do it?

There's no going back. Accept that, and go forward with enthusiasm and anticipation of better things to come. If you tell your attorney that you "used to do this" and you "used to have that," your attorney will probably shrug and tell you things are going to change.

If you lament to your friends, they may listen politely, but after a while even they'll stop listening. You can't bring back the past.

Life after divorce can be lonely and financially difficult. Many people feel disillusioned during the divorce process and after it's over. However, it's up to you how lonely, bereft, and denied you feel. Being preoccupied with the past is only a method of stalling the future. Don't sacrifice your future by immersing yourself in your past. Make new friends, find new hobbies, and get on with your life. You'll be surprised how good it feels. The attractions of your old life will slowly fade.

Learn from your past mistakes and set your sails for the new seas ahead.

Comparing your divorce to other people's can be dangerous.

Beware of the temptation to compare your divorce to divorces in films, books, TV shows, or the divorce of a friend, a celebrity, or even a fictional character.

"I watch reruns of *L.A. Law,* and Arnie Becker makes the spouse fold in one episode."

"I watched the OJ Simpson murder trial, and if his lawyer could get him acquitted, you should be able to get me everything I want and more."

"I saw *The War of the Roses,* and I want to make Barbara Rose look as if she was just toying with her husband."

Every divorce case has its own personality. No two cases are the same even though they may have aspects in common. Every case is unique, as is every result.

Sure, you should ask questions and can learn from another person's divorce, but the similarities you observe may be misleading. There are often legally significant subtleties that make your case different. Because of the personalities of the parties and their attorneys, the results can be very different in divorces with similar facts. Ask your attorney for specific advice relating to *your* divorce.

Barbara Rose, Arnie Becker, and OJ Simpson aren't worrying about you, so don't invest energy in what they did. Move forward in a realistic manner with your own case.

Rambling on and on to your attorney is a big mistake. Instead, sum up and condense your points.

Time is money. Every time you talk to your attorney, it costs money. Your attorney is billing you by the minute. Be prepared *before* you talk to your attorney. Have notes organized about what you want to discuss. The more concise and bottom-line you can be, the better. Take notes when you meet with your attorney and bring your notes to each meeting so that you can quickly and efficiently ask your questions, make your points, and give your input.

Prepare a list of questions so that you don't think of things to ask *after* you hang up the phone. If you need to refer to documents, have them available rather than putting your attorney on hold while you run around the house looking for the piece of paper that has the information you want.

Being succinct and organized with your attorney is good practice for if and when you have to testify in court. Your attorney's patience will wear thin if you can't get to the point. Even more alarming, your wallet will wear thin.

Don't stay with an attorney who is not responsive to your questions, needs, or problems.

If you feel your attorney is not responding to you, have an open talk with him or her about your concerns. Some attorneys don't communicate well or enough. This makes it difficult to know if your attorney is on top of your case.

This is not the time for blind loyalty.

If you talk to your attorney, and you still don't feel he or she is responsive or prepared, interview other lawyers to make sure your concerns are reasonable. Explore whether other counsel will be more capable of answering your questions, handling your case, and meeting your needs.

This is the rest of your life; you need someone who is in your corner.

Your relationship with your lawyer is like another marriage, and in some respects, it's no different than the one to your spouse: the longer you stay together, the harder it is to separate. The closer you are to trial, the more financially complicated and burdensome it becomes to bring in new counsel. So do yourself a favor. Change lawyers as soon as you can if yours is not doing the job.

Never assume you know the law.

After years of watching television lawyers, some of us think we're Perry Mason and know how to try a case. Not likely. Just because we watched Cousin Henry go through his divorce doesn't mean we know all the ropes. Because your neighbor is a lawyer and tells you his war stories, you may think you know how the law works. Trust us. Your confidence is misplaced.

Many people have misconceptions about the law. That's not the problem. The problem occurs when people *act* on those misconceptions or don't find out how the law specifically applies to their case.

Although your input is crucial, your lawyer must determine how the law applies to the facts of your case.

You don't know the ins and outs, and you don't know the law. That is what you're paying your lawyer to know. Instead of second-guessing him or her, have your attorney educate you and leave the lawyering to your lawyer.

While in court recently, a party was screaming at his attorney, "You tell that judge he's stupid. You tell that judge he doesn't know what he's doing. I know how much money I should be paying. If you won't tell him, I will." The attorney calmly withdrew as counsel from the case, the party returned to court, gave the court "a piece of his mind," and within half an hour was escorted out of the courtroom in handcuffs.

Using your attorney as a therapist is a bad idea.

Some family law attorneys have mastered hand-holding, but that doesn't mean they have any better insight than your next-door neighbor or your butcher as to when you're going to laugh again.

Make sure you're asking your attorney for *legal* advice. If you have a psychological issue, ask a mental health professional. Your attorney is not qualified to answer that type of question. Although your attorney may genuinely like you and be interested in your welfare, and you may want to rely on his or her advice, psychology is not your attorney's area of expertise.

The reality is that psychological problems often are a significant factor in your divorce. However, your attorney's job is to use the facts in the legal arena, not implement a solution for psychological issues. Your attorney must have all the facts. So tell your attorney, "My spouse drinks." The attorney will use that information to get you protection. But it is not your attorney to whom you should turn to get advice on either coping with your spouse's drinking problems or getting your spouse help with the problem.

Remember, you're being billed by the hour, and your attorney is probably a lot more expensive than a therapist.

Don't move out of your house voluntarily without having first spoken to an attorney.

Unless you are in fear of physical harm, moving out of the house without first speaking to an attorney is almost always a bad idea.

Many people rush to move out because they "can't take it anymore." They fail to consider what will follow. Your divorce is not unlike chess. You need to plan a couple of moves (no pun intended) in advance.

It may seem attractive to just pack your bags and leave in a huff, but such an impetuous act rarely is beneficial. Moving out of the house will dramatically impact your financial picture.

If you move out and rent a new place, you will have to come up with money for rent and the security deposit. If you own the home in which you reside, a move can have significant and costly tax ramifications. In either case, you will have to pay to have your belongings moved and have your telephone and utilities installed.

Consider: there will be two households which must be supported on the money previously supporting one.

From a strategic vantage, moving out can cost you leverage in negotiations. Perhaps your spouse would like you to move out as badly as you would like to leave. Your attorney may be able to negotiate some benefit for you in exchange for your agreement to move.

Don't start decorating your new home until you've gotten the green light from your lawyer.

Angry outbursts may forever alienate your spouse.

You may know the buttons to push, but think long and hard before pushing them. You can't take back words said in anger, and certain words will never be forgotten nor forgiven.

There are any number of reasons why you should not strike out in anger:

- If you want to reconcile, you will be sorry you wounded your spouse. You may say something that will boomerang to hurt you.
- You can turn a friend into an enemy, or you may cut the lines of communication.
- You can turn a civilized dispute into a war. That will undoubtedly make your divorce more expensive and more difficult on every level.

You don't have to want to stay married, nor do you have to like your spouse. But there is absolutely no constructive purpose served by outbursts. They will ensure that your spouse will be forever alienated and adopt the state of mind that "I'll die before I settle with you."

Never use your children as pawns.

It can't be said often enough: Divorce is between you and your spouse. Your children are not getting divorced. Don't use them to manipulate or "guilt" your spouse, act as go-betweens, or hurt your soon-to-be-ex. Your children's welfare is in your hands.

There are no worse reasons for a custody fight than to hurt your spouse.

There is no worse way to talk to your spouse than through your children.

One of the surest ways to damage your children is telling them all the things that are wrong with their *other* parent.

To estrange her daughters from their father, a mother told them he was refusing to contribute to their private school tuition and would pay nothing for their college. When the girls learned that he was actually paying their tuition, they moved in with him. Their mother really learned what it was like to lose her children's trust.

When you use your children, you become the villain and your children become the victims. Don't do it.

Avoid confessions that may later come back to haunt you.

We can't make it simpler. If it's something that can adversely impact your divorce litigation or if it's something you don't want your spouse to know, button up.

Whether it's about money, drugs, or alcohol abuse, a significant other, or any of myriad controversial subjects, don't talk with your spouse about anything you may later wish your spouse didn't know.

This advice is not limited to discussions with your spouse. It includes conversations with friends, joint therapy with your spouse, mediation and conciliation sessions, and even talks with your relatives.

While it is important to have a support system during the difficult period of divorce, remember that certain relationships may change over time. An outpouring of confidences or information you disclosed with the expectation that it would go no further may be innocently repeated—to your detriment. Without understanding the significance and the potential ramifications, your child or a well-intentioned friend or relative may echo your words to your spouse.

The protection you think you have in settings such as conciliation sessions or in joint therapy may be illusory. If your words are repeated, often there is no recourse. Distinguish this from discussions with your attorney, which are strictly confidential.

No amount of promises about confidentiality can protect you. While in therapy, our client told her therapist about undisclosed cash in her safe deposit box. When the therapist's notes were sub poenaed on an unrelated issue, the client was abashed and her husband was delighted about her revelation of her cash stash.

Anything you say may, can, and perhaps will be used against you later. If you *must* talk, be cautious to whom you confide.

Denigrating your spouse to your children creates major problems.

It's absolutely not acceptable. No matter how big a heel he is, no matter how horrid she is. It is imperative that you not tell your children about the contempt you feel for your spouse. Your children will suffer.

Your children love both of you and don't want to be in the middle. You shouldn't put them there. This is not to say that you should lie to your children. For example, if their father does not pick them up for visitation, you must be honest and tell them he isn't coming. However, to say things such as "He's so stupid, he probably forgot about you" will only make your children feel bad about themselves and their situation. Your children gain nothing by hearing a diatribe against the other parent.

Don't fool yourself. If you tear down your spouse, *your* relationship with your children will be adversely impacted. And a judge won't like it, either. It is not inconceivable for custody to be modified or even lost if you persist in that behavior. No matter how you toss the dice, you'll come up short when you vilify the other parent.

The amount of harm and confusion you cause your children by this conduct is unlimited. As difficult as it is at times, the best approach may be the old adage: If you don't have something nice to say, don't say anything at all.

Also remember: If you speak about the other parent with respect, you are teaching your children respect.

Inflexible or overreaching demands are counter-productive.

The smartest approach to divorce is to recognize that both sides benefit when everyone is open to compromise. Cases are resolved less expensively, less acrimoniously, and more quickly.

Whether it is caused by anger, despair, or lack of any other options, it is ill-advised for you to dig in your heels and refuse to budge when you take an unreasonable position. The results can be disastrous and costly. In some jurisdictions a judge will order you to pay your spouse's fees because of the unreasonableness of your demands.

On the flip side, it may be your spouse who won't or can't negotiate reasonably. Some people can't take yes for an answer. Others want revenge. Others just want to stay involved with their spouse even if it's through attorneys. If your spouse's demands are unrealistic and no amount of information will persuade him or her to change position, accept that fact and try the case. However, even if you believe your spouse can't negotiate reasonably, make a realistic settlement proposal. You may come up with acceptable solutions that your spouse hadn't even considered. If your proposal is fair, the opposing attorney may be able to guide your spouse into settlement, and you will benefit. With settlement you almost always end up with more of what you want because you can tailor the deal to your particular priorities.

To evaluate whether your demands are inflexible or unreasonable, consider your likelihood of success if you were to present that same demand to a judge.

Don't think that if you give in on a major "deal point," your spouse will come back.

Don't bet on it. A lot of people have, and they've lost.

Beware if your spouse tells you he or she will come back only if you agree to particular demands that you adamantly oppose. A "take it or leave it" ultimatum should be a tipoff that your spouse is only concerned about meeting his or her own agenda, as opposed to working toward a common goal. If your spouse has no intention of coming back under any circumstances, you're just negotiating against yourself if you give in.

Divorce is never over one issue. A single concession can't be a cure-all for your marital discord. Reconciliation means compromising and working together to repair your marriage. Usually, one side's complete capitulation is not the solution. It creates winners and losers, and the "loser" feels resentment if the sacrifice isn't appreciated, which it rarely is.

Being a doormat may work short term, but in the end your spouse will leave again and walk all over you. Don't be held hostage to your marriage.

You may not have to lose your home.
There are usually many reasons that keeping your home is a good idea. Chances are that it's in a neighborhood where you like to live, is near friends and work, and is affordable. Keeping it also allows you to avoid the expense of moving and the difficulty of qualifying for a loan on a new place. If you have children, staying in your home will be one less adjustment for them. It is always preferable if children do not have to change schools and start making new friends right on the heels of adjusting to their parents no longer being partners.

Sometimes keeping your home can be accomplished rather simply—by giving your spouse another asset in exchange. Don't be afraid to look into what it would take to buy out your spouse's interest in the house. It may not be as much money as you imagine. Your spouse may be inclined to discount the amount because he or she will receive it tax-free.

If you own your home, keep the mortgage current. The damage to your credit from losing your home will haunt you for years, long after your divorce is over. Furthermore, there may be substantial income tax penalties if your house goes into foreclosure.

Your decision to keep or lose your home must be guided by reasoned financial, rather than emotional, considerations.

There is no way you can successfully outsmart or lie to your attorney and the other side.
You had *better* be successful, because once you're caught, your credibility is ruined for the duration. And don't kid yourself, you *will* be caught.

In our experience the only people who lie and get away with it are those who do it professionally. If you are not one of those people, don't even try it. In your lifetime you probably won't be involved in the divorce process more than three times. Judges and attorneys are involved in hundreds or even thousands of divorces. The system, clumsy as it may sometimes seem, is calculated to discover liars and punish them.

Divorce is a little like going to the doctor for an annual physical. You're poked and probed everywhere. Discovery of the malady is virtually inevitable.

Lying under oath is foolish and arrogant. No one knows you better than your spouse. Take our word for it—whatever story you tell has been tried before.

There is no benefit in lying or failing to disclose information to your attorney. You are jeopardizing your own interests. Even if the facts are bad, attorneys can assist you when they know the truth. You may not get what you want, but you'll get what's fair. If you lie and your attorney finds out the truth from the other side or in court, your advocate can rarely help you. You will suffer the consequences.

A woman told her husband and her own attorney that she couldn't work because of a neck injury. She religiously saw her doctor and wore her neck brace. Her husband, however, was suspicious. When the court was considering the wife's request for alimony, the husband produced a video documenting his wife carrying heavy boxes up two flights of stairs, bowling, and line dancing. There was little the wife's attorney could do in the face of such damning evidence.

Your spouse and his or her attorney will find it difficult, if not impossible, to continue negotiations with a liar. After all, how can they trust anything you say?

If you lie, lawyers will withdraw from representing you. If you lie under oath, you have committed perjury, which is a crime. When you're caught lying, the judge may find all of your testimony suspect and be inclined to rule more favorably for your spouse.

Invariably, you end up the big loser when you lie.

Don't have your date or "significant other" answer the phone at your home.

This is a piece of commonsense advice. Jealousy is often an element in marriage and divorce. Why look for trouble? This may not be a problem for your soon-to-be-ex, but on the other hand, the odds are that it will be. This seemingly insignificant act can move your divorce from a small skirmish to out-and-out war.

If custody is an issue, your spouse will inevitably find a way to turn the telephone "incident" into another reason that you are an inappropriate parent. Don't ask how something so innocent can be turned into a detriment for your children. Trust us. Your spouse will do it, and you'll pay your lawyer endlessly to remedy something that you could have avoided easily.

The best way to preserve your privacy is for *you* to preserve it.

Competing with your spouse for your children's love and approval is self-defeating.

It's a lose-lose strategy. Your children won't end up loving you any more. They will be subjected to stress, conflict, and confusion, and you will end up resentful and unfulfilled. Competing may seem the best way, but if it works at all, it is only in the short run. With children, long-term commitment and love will prevail.

Don't underestimate your children, either. Even when you enforce rules, children know when they're loved. On the flip side, children may happily collect the bribes, but they know when they're being bought. And to what end? Your children will be a lot healthier if they believe they are loved by *both* parents.

Keep your children's needs as the first priority. You don't need to compete. Your children already love you and always will.

Rushing to file your tax returns alone may backfire.

Don't rush to file separate tax returns because you think it's to your advantage or because you've vowed never to have anything to do with your spouse again.

Consult an accountant about the advantages and disadvantages of filing jointly *before* you make any decisions. With respect to income taxes, divorcing spouses may find they have a common goal that can be accomplished with a little bit of cooperation. Often spouses can save money or even be entitled to refunds by filing joint returns. Perhaps your spouse will pay you one-half of the amount saved by filing jointly or give you some other concession because your filing jointly will save money.

Filing jointly, however, subjects you to liability for any wrongdoing committed by your spouse on the tax return. This potential exposure must not be overlooked.

Remember, filing tax returns is a business decision, not an emotional one. First get all of the relevant information, *then* act.

Be cautious of groups that say they want to "protect" you but are really nothing more than a forum for spouse and lawyer bashing.

The nineties is the age of groups. If you want to get in touch with your former life or get help for a pet with a personality disorder, never fear, there's a group for you. There's nothing wrong with groups as long as you know what you're getting into.

Groups of disenchanted people may entice you with empathy

for your grievances but offer no positive direction. For example, there are groups whose philosophy is to get custody away from fathers or to make mothers go to work. These groups are not objective and not motivated to take *your* particular facts into consideration and give *you* helpful advice. They frequently overstate their position. Reliance on their representations may cause you harm and expense.

There are also groups that serve no function other than to bash your spouse, attorneys, expert witnesses, and psychologists. Remember, these are forums in which only one viewpoint is presented or tolerated. Accordingly, you have no way of knowing if the speaker's position is justified. More significant, it is important to ask yourself how you are served by listening to others rant about the "hateful" atrocities perpetrated on them by their spouse, their spouse's attorney, or even their own attorney.

Far more constructive is finding groups that guide you in the direction of what *you* should do.

There are many constructive groups for the recently divorced, providing support and information for the varied problems that confront the newly single person or the now single parent.

Don't get swept up in a wave of malcontents. Find the right group for you.

5

DO'S, DON'TS, AND MAYBES

Ten Commandments of Love

Don't put on fifteen pounds from stress and aggravation.
The great sugar rush will only get you so far. Eating may soothe you temporarily, but if you want to know real stress and aggravation, try dieting during a divorce. Try to stick to your normal eating patterns.

Think of divorce as a good excuse to look as good as you did before you married your spouse. You'll feel better if you look better, so be your own best friend and take care of yourself.

Do assume your spouse will look in your home for any useful evidence. Safeguard letters from a significant other, correspondence from your attorney, or anything else that could harm you.
Your spouse may not have been a snoop in the past, but now that you're divorcing, look who's turning into Jessica Fletcher. It's a jungle, and it rapidly becomes survival of the fittest. A spouse who sees an opportunity to learn something or get an advantage will take it.

While moving out at the time of separation, a prominent female physician left behind an old magazine that graphically documented how she had paid for medical school—posing in the buff. Under the circumstances she felt more motivated to cooperate with her spouse in settling the case.

If you want to give something away, do it on your own terms, not because you were foolish enough to leave documents lying around the house or tucked away in your underwear drawer, the same place you've hidden things for the last ten years of marriage.

There is absolutely no reason that your spouse should be privy to the communications between you and your attorney. Stow those documents in a safe place—perhaps out of the house altogether. The same goes for private correspondence with a lover or business associate, or practically anyone else for that matter.

If you are still in the same house with your spouse, consider renting a post office box for confidential communications or having your mail sent to a close friend or relative. If you're going to throw away correspondence, do it somewhere other than at your own home! An estranged spouse isn't beyond taping together bits of torn letters to see what you're hiding.

Do things that reduce stress.

Do whatever it takes to get you through the day, the week, and the year, and keeps you from obsessing about your divorce. Divorce makes you feel out of control because, in fact, you are out of control. Go to the movies, bake, get a massage, read, surf the Internet, play sports, exercise, sew, tinker in the garage, plan a weekend away. The options are limitless.

Even those of you who initiated the process will suffer. Divorce is just one of those miserable times in life, and the best thing you can do for yourself is find distractions that make you feel less stressed.

If you reduce tension, you will be more productive when you do have to focus on your divorce. You'll find that when you are participating in activities that reduce stress, you think more clearly and find solutions to problems that seemed insoluble before.

Don't sign documents given to you by your spouse without first showing them to your lawyer. Don't even sign documents handed to you by your own lawyer without first reading them.

Never sign a document without reading it. *Never* sign a document with blanks to be filled in later. *Never* sign anything your spouse gives you during your divorce or in anticipation of divorce unless your lawyer has reviewed it, approved it, explained the significance of the document, and advised you to sign it. Your spouse is your adversary. Don't sign the document and *then* ask your lawyer about it. You may have taken an irrevocable step.

While eating pasta in a restaurant and talking about how to save their marriage, our client was presented with a document by her spouse. He asked her to sign it, claiming it had something to do with attorneys, "and don't worry, it's nothing important." She almost signed it, then told him she had to go to the bathroom. While in the ladies' room, she called us and read the document, a power of attorney that would have made her husband her "attorney in fact" with the right to sign her name to anything. She flushed the document down the toilet, left the restaurant, and arrived at our office to file for divorce.

We learned this when we were young: Don't sign a document without reading it first. It was good advice then, and it still is.

Don't lose sight of the fact that you and your spouse are no longer on the same team. Do not assume that just because you always signed everything he or she put under your nose, it's fine to continue with that conduct. It's not. Even if you trust your spouse, err on the side of caution. Read whatever you are being asked to sign, and take it to your attorney to be reviewed.

Even documents prepared by your attorney should be read before being signed by you. Lawyers have been known to get information wrong. Often you are signing under penalty of perjury. Ultimately, it is your responsibility to make sure the document is completely correct. An ounce of prevention is worth a pound of cure.

Don't go on a spending spree, no matter how tempting.

A client bought three fur coats in one afternoon. Another flew to Paris for lunch and then flew home. You say it will never be you, but you might surprise yourself. Don't.

The rude awakening is that in most states it is your responsibility to pay obligations incurred by you after separation. In other words, the bills you run up may be deducted from your settlement. Even large debts run up *in contemplation* of divorce may end up becoming your sole responsibility.

As good as it may feel to go on a spree, the rush will disappear quickly when you have to pay the piper. Furthermore, such conduct is frequently in violation of restraining orders and will no doubt make you look bad in front of the judge to whom your case is assigned. A little self-control goes a long way.

Don't get hooked watching the weather channel—things aren't better anywhere else.

The grass may look greener, but it's a mirage. Confront the issues before you. Take responsibility by dealing with your problems, and they will be resolved. Ignoring them, running away, or burying your head in the sand will only give you momentary respite. Your difficulties will still be there when you resurface.

Do figure out whom you can trust before you go talking to friends and soon-to-be former relatives. You may be surprised to see who will pop up to testify against you later.

You are guaranteed to learn who your friends are when you go through a divorce. You may find out at the start, or you may learn along the way. The problem is that sometimes you don't find out until you're deep into the process, and by then you may have confided in exactly the wrong person.

As certain as you are that this will never happen to you, the odds are that it will happen in one out of two cases.

Do take notes when you have meetings with your lawyer and jot down questions and ideas as they come to you.

You think you'll remember, but you won't. "What did my lawyer say?" you'll ask yourself. "Did my lawyer say I *should* or I *shouldn't* tell my spouse? I just can't remember." Don't rely on your memory. Write it down. Divorce increases stress, and stress affects your ability to remember. Take notes. It's easier and less expensive to take notes than to call your lawyer and ask the same question again.

Take the practical, economical approach and write down your questions and ideas as you think of them. The more organized you are when you walk into your lawyer's office, the less time you'll spend there and the less time you'll be billed for. If you think you can remember every question and idea you have, you're wrong. This is a time when you have a lot on your mind. Jot down notes so you don't forget.

Do make a police report if there is abuse—and do follow through.

Don't make excuses for your spouse. Don't say it will never happen again or that it never happened before. It shouldn't have happened *once*.

Don't believe that it will only be worse if you report the incident.

Make a police report and follow through with whatever needs to be done. In some states your spouse can't be ordered out of the house without a hearing unless there is physical abuse. Don't make it your word against your spouse's word. Get an official record of the incident, have pictures taken of injuries, and put your evidence where your spouse can't destroy it.

In a rather unusual turn of events, a husband told us that he had been beaten by his wife over the last few years. We asked him if he had made a police report, seen a physician, or confided in any friends or coworkers. His answer was no to all questions. Based on his wife's denial of the accusations, the judge refused to order his wife out of the house. It may be humiliating, it may be the toughest thing you ever do, but if there's abuse, report it.

Nothing you do prevents your spouse from getting the help she or he needs.

As difficult as it may be, "I'm so sorry" is not enough. Once you let someone get away with violence of any kind, it's an open invitation to do it again.

Don't involve the children in conversations, arguments, or decisions about them. Do not discuss the particulars of divorce with your children, and do not use them as mediators or go-betweens. Your divorce is between you and your spouse. Do not put your children in the middle.

Your children should not see or hear, much less participate, in any arguments. Under no circumstances should they mediate arguments between you and your spouse, nor should you use them as a messenger service to pass messages to your spouse. Bringing your children into the discussions and decisions will only slow their healing process and confuse them. Worse, it may lead them to anguish about their perceived responsibility for the marital breakup. The problem snowballs when children think they can make things better. And when it doesn't improve, your kids have yet another issue to wonder and worry about: Could *they* have done something more or different to mend the rift between their parents? Involving your children is a no-win situation.

Don't become abusive to yourself. Don't convince yourself that alcohol, drugs, overeating, or not eating at all is going to help. When all else fails, the most likely victim for us to beat up is ourselves. It's sad but true.

Doing *anything* in excess is not the answer. And doing some things *at all* may not be the answer, either.

It's very important to take care of yourself physically. Eat sensibly, get rest, and establish some kind of sensible routine. Eventually you are going to have to deal with reality. The long-term negative effects of abusing yourself during the divorce will no doubt be more detrimental than anything you experience as a result of the divorce.

Make sure that you are as kind to yourself as you would be to your best friend. This is the time to do unto you.

Don't use the same lawyer.
It may seem an appealing and inexpensive way to handle things, but using the same lawyer as your spouse is a major mistake.

One lawyer cannot equally represent conflicting interests. For example, if you say you need a high amount of monthly support and your spouse wants to pay as little as possible, how can one lawyer who is supposed to be an advocate for each of you resolve those competing interests?

Each party should obtain separate counsel and get separate advice. Although the goal may be to work things out, it can't be done without first understanding your options as well as the best and worst case scenarios. Cases can be resolved amicably with each side having separate representation. It's important that you understand your rights as well as your responsibilities in the divorce setting.

It should be noted that even in mediated cases it is frequently recommended that each party have independent counsel.

In the long run, no one will save money by using one lawyer. Courts look askance and may throw out agreements drafted by one lawyer for both parties, and then everyone has to start all over again.

Do spend time with people who give you a positive feeling about yourself and your future.

Have you ever noticed that some people have a positive approach to almost everything, and others see doom and gloom everywhere? Well, now is the time to surround yourself with some of those positive people.

Divorce can be one of life's more depressing experiences. Instead of wallowing in it, find people who will make you feel encouraged, optimistic, even excited about your future and about yourself.

Your past is over, and your future has all kinds of possibilities.

Do try to resolve with your spouse any issues about which there is no dispute or where the value is less than the cost to litigate.

Sometimes when we put the gloves on, we forget that we don't necessarily have to use them. So use some common sense. The more issues agreed upon by you and your spouse, the better it is. Still, don't forget to check with your attorney before you commit in writing to any deal.

If you listen carefully, you may discover that you and your spouse are saying the same thing. In other words, if there is no argument on an issue, get it in writing and move on.

Try to sit down with your spouse and work out the smaller issues, such as the division of furniture and furnishings, automobiles, family photos, and knickknacks.

Refer to the *Kelley Blue Book* to assist in the valuation of automobiles. You can divide furniture by auction, by alternate selection, or by having one party take the furniture and the other party an agreed-upon value in exchange.

Don't spend $1,500 in lawyer time to argue about a $50 issue. Before you say you'd never do that, step back and examine the issues in your case one more time to make sure you're not already doing just that without realizing it.

Don't take out your anger and despair on innocents—your kids, friends, family, the local butcher.

We know you feel awful, but you can't take it out on the world. It's always easiest to take our anger out on the ones we know won't reject us, who will understand. But don't do it. Use your friends and family for support and guidance. Don't lose your patience with your children just because you've lost it with your spouse or the system or your spouse's attorney. Don't get irritable with a coworker because *you're* feeling irritable. Stay cordial with the people who inhabit your day-to-day existence.

If you can't curb your anger, at least channel it constructively. Give your attorney the information he or she needs to be able to get you the best results possible. If you're still angry, read books, seek professional help, or take up a hobby.

Your anger is like a lion: You can't let it out of its cage unless the lion tamer is on duty, and you never want to put your children or your family or friends into the lion's cage. Protect the innocent bystanders from that lion.

Don't alienate the people who love and support you.

Don't withhold court-ordered payments as punishment or leverage, and do pay support on time.

When the court orders you to pay support, it is not a commercial transaction like shopping for sports equipment. You are paying money, but you're not getting something back. The bottom line is that your obligation to pay ordered support is *independent* of all other obligations. The order is not a request for you to consider; it is a mandate.

There are almost no excuses to justify late payment or non-payment of support. If you don't pay or you pay late, you will lose points in the legal process and run the risk of wage attachment, enforcement proceedings, and possibly criminal action. It will, at best, cost you more money. At worst, you could be looking at the inside of a jail cell.

If you're trying to make a point with your spouse, do it in a different way.

If you need the support to be lowered or eliminated, file for that relief. If the court agrees with you, your support payment will be decreased. But don't decide to lower or eliminate the payment without the court's blessing. It's not as if you're channel surfing. Here, the remote has been programmed for you.

If you have an emotional block about writing a check each month, try writing one for three months' support and pay it in advance. That reduces the irritation to four times a year. If you have a really good relationship with a bank, for a fee the bank may agree to issue the check once a month by automatic withdrawal.

Don't fight about paying support at all or paying it on time. Just do it.

Do change the locks on your house when your spouse is legally out.

Ever had the feeling that things aren't arranged in your drawer the way you left them? It's a feeling you might find yourself experiencing if you don't change the locks.

One never knows if your soon-to-be former spouse is going to respect the fact that you are exclusively and temporarily or permanently residing in the family residence. As much as you may trust him or her, there is a great benefit and no downside to err on the side of caution. Change the locks, change the security codes, and don't forget to call the security company and let them know the new numbers and that your spouse is no longer allowed in the house. If you are now in possession of the property, there is no reason for anyone other than you to have the keys.

Spouses do enter uninvited and look for information, remove objects, and wreak destruction. Rather than saying it will never happen to you, ensure that it doesn't.

Don't use your former spouse as a financial adviser when the marriage is over.

We know you may still trust your ex and think you won't get a bum steer, but don't do it. The reasons are many and varied, and more than one may apply to you.

The marriage is over, and it's time to make a fresh start. A fresh start doesn't mean relying on your old standby, your spouse (or former or soon-to-be-former spouse). The hardest way to move forward is to continue living in the past. Find someone new to help you with financial advice.

Get in the habit of having a private life, particularly with respect to your ex. Private means that your financial affairs are your business, Not the business of the person to whom you used to be married.

You and your former spouse have potential, if not actual, conflicts of interest.

Letting your former spouse into your financial life is also inviting comments such as "You shouldn't spend so much money on blah blah" or "I think you're in a position to contribute more toward our children's xyz."

Professional financial advisers have no conflict with you. Choose one of them and pay them. If they make a mistake, you have legal recourse. If you get angry with them, you can fire them without any emotional involvement. Not so with your former spouse.

It's not a great leap from telling you how to invest your money to just telling you what to do.

Don't settle your case just because you crave closure.

Settlements made in haste because "I just can't take it anymore" are more often than not regretted later. Hang in there. Impatience ranks high as a *bad* reason to settle a case.

Don't make revenge your goal.

Revenge hurts the one who seeks it. Revenge often proves to be expensive and ultimately unfulfilling. "Getting even" is a plot line better left to the screwball comedies of the thirties. Expend your energy in a more productive fashion. If you are obsessing about revenge, consider the possibility that you are still emotionally involved with your spouse.

Your goal should be to walk out of the marriage with the best settlement that can be accomplished under your circumstances and within the law.

Do try to view the situation from your spouse's standpoint.

There are two sides to every story. The only way you are going to change your spouse's viewpoint is by trying to understand where your spouse is coming from. Jump into his or her perspective so that you can better understand that position and figure out the best way to sell the alternative. The possibility does exist that you've dug your heels in on the wrong side or that there is a solution that meets the needs of both of you. Looking at the issues from your spouse's point of view may enable you to see where you're off track or where the compromise lies. Sometimes two people in conflict really agree in principle, although their proposals sound different.

If you understand your spouse's position, you may be able to find areas of agreement that can be used as a springboard to settlement.

Don't let yourself be goaded because your spouse knows your hot spots.

Let's face it. Who knows better than your spouse what makes you crazy? Armed with this knowledge, be ready when your spouse aims for that nerve. Don't jump. Don't scream. Don't fall apart. Just ignore it and proceed. If you don't, in addition to feeling out of control, you'll hurt your negotiating position.

Don't let your spouse set you off. Be particularly careful if your spouse is attempting to goad you into a situation in which your behavior is being closely scrutinized. We've seen spouses trying to provoke their mate in court when a judge is present. Another common place for this to occur is during child custody evaluations where a psychologist or psychiatrist is present and intensely alert to behavior and reactions. The damage is compounded by the fact that the comment or action triggering your explosion will be something that appears innocuous to the observer.

So if you see your spouse trying to provoke you, take a deep breath and stay calm.

Maybe . . . reconsider your position if you think the marriage can be saved.

Never say never. There are marriages that can be saved.

Just because you've started the process doesn't mean you can't stop it or, at least, put it on hold if you and your spouse make that choice. Don't forget to inform your attorneys of this decision immediately.

Set aside your pride and forget the motivation that got you into the lawyer's office. If you still love your spouse and you think your spouse may still love you, there's hope. Maybe think about going for it. It may mean counseling, a spontaneous vacation together, or an intimate dinner to talk things out. But what's your downside? You'll end up getting divorced? Well, that's where you were anyway. The pluses of the upside are boundless.

6

GOING THROUGH THE PROCESS

It's My Party

Take a deep breath and come to terms with the fact that one of you must file and serve the papers.

One of you has to be the first to take the plunge. If you want to get the divorce process started and embark on the path through the legal system, either you or your spouse has to file the necessary paperwork.

You don't get divorced by talking about it or wishing for it. There is a formal procedure that must be followed either through an attorney, with the assistance of a paralegal, or by educating yourself as to what must be done. Each state has its own label for the document that must be filed, but whether it's called a petition, complaint, or something else, you won't get to the end without starting at the beginning. This is where it begins.

Once the papers are filed, the nonfiling spouse must be served or accept service of the papers so that both of you now have formal notice of the divorce and are "in the system."

Reconcile yourself to the fact that divorce is its own bureaucratic nightmare, and there is no way around the rules and regulations. Take that deep breath, grit your teeth, and do what you have to do.

Either through litigation or negotiation, interim arrangements must be made to maintain the status quo, preserve assets, define time periods during which the children will be with each parent, and provide financial assistance for the supported spouse and children.

You may be in emotional limbo for a long time, but the smart move is to remove uncertainty in other areas as quickly as possible after the divorce process begins.

It's almost impossible to predict how amicable the process will be. As a result, the best advice may seem like overkill, but it's wise to err on the side of caution.

Temporary orders are necessary to protect assets from disappearing or being dissipated before the case is over. These orders are necessary to protect debt from being run up.

Provision must be made for your children. Where will they reside? Who will be responsible for their care on specific days and at specific times? How will their expenses be paid? Who will take care of medical insurance, school lunches, allowances, clothes for the new school semester, and the rest of the endless list of costs one has for children? Whether by settlement or trial, temporary arrangements must be worked out for child support pending resolution of the case.

Decisions will have to be reached about who will continue to live in the family residence. Who will pay the mortgage, taxes, insurance, and maintenance? These issues must be dealt with immediately, not later.

If one spouse is earning considerably more than the other, should that spouse be paying support to the lower earner while the case is pending? Should one of you be contributing to the attorney's fees of the other? Should one of you be giving the other an accounting for a business or how an asset is being invested?

These are matters that must be explored immediately with a

competent family law attorney. Depending on the complexity of the issues in your case, there may be numerous interim orders that must be put in place to make sure your life and the lives of your children have as little upheaval as possible. This is not to say there won't be change. Remember, the income that once supported one household may now have to support two. On the other hand, a spouse who is a low earner or nonearner should not be in a position where she or he has to beg the other for money, nor should one spouse be pleading with the other for the right to see the children.

Getting some temporary arrangement in place is done differently in various states. It's best to consult an attorney and do so before irreparable damage has been done by your spouse.

If your spouse takes your life savings and gambles it away in a despondent pique, a judge may order that you're owed half of the squandered money. But it's your problem, not the judge's, to collect it. Wouldn't it have been easier to have anticipated and avoided the problem by "freezing" the money?

Discovery, the investigative and information-gathering process of divorce, must be commenced to obtain the information necessary to settle or litigate your case.

Never go to a gunfight with a knife. Don't try to settle a case without all of the information about your assets, liabilities, and respective incomes. This is foolish and ill-advised.

There's no need to panic because you're in the dark about what you own and what you owe. The law provides methods by which your spouse must disclose, under penalty of perjury, all the information he or she knows.

The methods vary, but they are many and they are effective. Questions can be posed to your spouse in writing and orally. The responses must be returned, truthfully, in the same form.

For those who believe that no truth will ever pass through the lips of their spouse, the law provides you with the right to serve subpoenas on witnesses as diverse as employers, bank officers, neighbors, relatives, stockbrokers, teachers, and virtually any individual or institution that may have information pertaining to the issues of your divorce.

A client whose husband claimed he was not working came to us about a divorce. She was financially supporting the family by working from 4:00 A.M. to 5:00 P.M., and taking care of the children and all the household chores. Her husband said he simply couldn't do anything around the house because he felt so ill and depressed. However, he did go out every day for a walk. Through discovery, documents were obtained showing he had earned over $750,000 in the stock market while he was "out for a walk" and that he had hidden the money in someone else's name. The process provided the tools to uncover buried treasures.

It's nice to trust your spouse, but even in the most trusting situations, it's usually a good idea to conduct discovery to evaluate your position intelligently and assess the merits of any settlement proposal.

To determine the amount of financial assistance for the supported spouse and the children, if any, both sides must prepare income and expense information.
More forms. They differ from state to state, but the concept is the same. Both sides are entitled to know and should know each other's income and monthly expenses. Start getting that information together.

It's impossible to discuss support and other issues intelligently without having a good idea of income and expenses. Pay stubs, W-2s, 1099s, and tax returns are all routinely reviewed and exchanged in connection with divorces. Get that information together and give it to your attorney. It's also not a bad idea to start keeping records of your monthly expenses. Not only will your attorney need that information, but it can also help you understand where a budget can be tightened if necessary.

Unfortunately, not all cases are straightforward. Experts may be hired to determine if there is additional income, hidden income, or assets. In some instances tax returns and W-2s are not complete and accurate reflections of what your spouse earns. There may be money received "under the table." Or it may be that your spouse owns a business and runs personal expenses, "perks," through the business as if they were business expenses. In determining your spouse's income for receipt or payment of support, these perks are added back to income. Sometimes an employer may allow benefits to your spouse that are not reflected as income but should be. If you fall into these or similar categories, it may be necessary to retain a forensic accountant or some other expert to assist in the process of computing income available for support versus the income shown on an income tax return.

But be careful what you wish for. While you may want your lawyer to find that your spouse has considerably more income than he or she has revealed, such a discovery can have devastating tax ramifications. The IRS may be fascinated by your discovery. All of this needs to be discussed with your lawyer.

Having the IRS as your enemy can make your former spouse look like a pussycat.

The identity, ownership, and value of property must be established. In many cases this task is easy—the house, car, and furniture are typical. In other cases, however, the court must decide what property exists, what the values are, and how much of each asset is owned by each party.

Save yourself some time. Before you walk into a lawyer's office, put together a list consisting of the following: every asset you and your spouse own; in whose name these assets stand; the date on which they were acquired; the prices paid at the time of purchase; the current amount owed on each asset; the current value; and why you think the asset belongs to you, your spouse, or both of you.

With this information your attorney will have a head start. Give your attorney any papers in your possession documenting the answers to any of these questions. Ultimately, if you and your spouse are unable to reach an agreement, the court will decide. The court is not bound to accept the position of either party.

To protect you and your property, restraining orders can be issued by the court.

You don't need to live in fear; just open your mouth and tell your lawyer what you are afraid of. It's a good bet there's some kind of order to put most of your concerns to rest.

If you're fearful for your well-being, restraining orders can be obtained to prohibit violent conduct, harassment, stalking, and verbal abuse.

If you're worried about your children being kidnapped or removed from the city, restraining orders can be obtained to prevent children from being removed from a specific area.

If you're positive your spouse will dissipate assets, run up debt, or spend all your money, restraining orders can be obtained to prevent the concealment, dissipation, encumbrance, and transfer of assets, and acquisition of new debt in your name.

If you are terrified that insurance, whether medical, auto, or life, will be canceled, restraining orders can be obtained to prevent that from happening.

In some states some of these restraining orders automatically go into effect as soon as the other party is served. In others you must go to court to request these orders.

A wealthy Brazilian actress who also lived in the United States stalked out of court during the divorce trial and refused to return. Her husband obtained a judgment awarding him in excess of $8 million. Unfortunately, his attorney did not immediately obtain restraining orders to prevent his wife from withdrawing funds from bank accounts. The orders were issued a month later. Too late! Every dollar the wife had in the United States had already gone south.

Restraining orders can be obtained to right most of the wrongs you anticipate may come down the pike. Close the barn door before the horse gets out. But be careful. Don't be naive. Restraining orders only work if treated with the solemnity and respect they should be accorded. If your spouse thinks he or she is above the law, restraining orders are just a piece of paper.

If custody is contested, the court may require mandatory mediation or psychological evaluations.

Custody is the one area that is definitely not just about "the law." Judges have come to realize that in rendering custodial decisions, professional psychological assistance can be very useful and is often necessary. Many judges do not hesitate to avail themselves of all the resources out there to aid them.

In some states the court may require mandatory mediation. The hope is that a neutral mediator will help you and your spouse come up with an agreeable resolution so that it won't be necessary for the matter to be submitted to a judge.

If that fails, judges frequently look to an independent third party to formulate a more child-oriented approach to the problem. In some states a judge may appoint counsel for the children and ask those advocates to make recommendations based on their investigation.

Still other courts have panels of psychologists, social workers, and psychiatrists who conduct home studies and psychological evaluations. Judges frequently give the reports from these professionals more weight than testimony that may be biased or self-serving.

The important thing to keep in mind is that you, your life, your activities, and your attitude will be under a microscope if custody is an issue. Be prepared to put your best foot forward, whether an examination is done by an expert you have retained, one who is court appointed, or one who has been mutually designated by you and your spouse.

A word to the wise: The court usually won't get involved in your custodial arrangements if you and your spouse can work out a reasonable plan.

Decisions will have to be made about the retention of experts.

Divorce is like a ball game, and your lawyer is your coach. One of the important decisions that has to be made is what experts you will need, who they will be, and how they will be paid. You should give the "coach" your ideas about this and then sit back and listen to the game plan.

Do you need a forensic accountant, psychologist, real estate appraiser, pension plan actuary, or someone to value the baseball card collection?

By way of example, if there's a business owned by you and your spouse, a business appraiser may be needed to testify about its fair market value. Although you may have a good knowledge of the books and records or may even be the one running the business, your testimony as to its value is rife with problems. If you want to keep the business, you are obviously motivated to give it a low value. If you want to be bought out, the reverse would be the case.

The same problem can arise with many assets, such as the family residence, rental property, artwork, a boat, rare stamps, antiques, or a train collection. An expert appraiser in a particular area has a reputation to protect, one that has a life span beyond your case. Accordingly, he or she brings a neutrality to the appraisal that is lacking from your opinion.

Pension plans can be very tricky assets to value, and without an expert in the area, you may find yourself lost and overwhelmed.

An expert is not needed to appraise every item owned by you and your spouse, but it's important to have one when needed. Don't appraise your TV, but don't neglect the Tiffany lamp!

Depending on the complexity of your financial situation, consider whether or not you need to obtain tax advice from a specialist.

The one thing everyone agrees on is that no one understands taxes. Taxes are the Bermuda triangle of family law.

Some cases don't have complicated tax problems or a great need for tax analysis. But in other cases, it can be disastrous if the tax ramifications are not thoroughly understood and explored.

It's crucial to recognize the need for expert tax advice. Most family law attorneys have a passing knowledge of taxes, but if you need to scratch much deeper than the surface, it's a good idea to consult a specialist.

Talk about this with your lawyer. A good lawyer will often know when an expert is needed. For example, the payment of alimony has tax consequences. The retention of an asset, whether it is the family residence, pension plan, stock portfolio or income-producing property, has tax ramifications that should be understood before you agree to take the asset. Our client's husband agreed that his back child support would be paid from his half of the proceeds from the sale of the house. The bad news for him was that when the house was sold and the child support paid to our client, he received no money out of the house but was still liable for one-half of the tax on the gain from the sale of the house.

Some assets have loss carryforwards attached to them. Some assets have deductions that can be used by you and other expenses that are not deductible for income tax purposes. Some assets are taxed at lower rates than ordinary income, some at a higher rate. Your children are tax exemptions. Early withdrawals from pensions and IRA accounts have both tax and penalty consequences.

Taxes are everywhere you turn in divorces. Don't shrug this off as a nonissue for you. Don't decide to ignore taxes because they are just "too complicated." Talk about taxes with your attorney and, if appropriate, hire a tax specialist.

Taxes are truly an area where "forewarned is forearmed."

At some point you are going to have to understand the difference between what you believe is true and what can be proven and presented in court.

It's awfully nice to speak with conviction. And we know it's great to be absolutely right. But if you can't testify to it and back it up in a manner that makes it admissible in court, that and a token will get you on the subway. In other words, it's worthless.

One of the hardest things for people to get through their heads is that really, truly, absolutely for certain, positively knowing something, is not always enough. You may not be able to testify about what Martha told Harry even if Martha has repeatedly told you she said it. The "something" must be admissible evidence before a judge can even begin to consider if what you are so certain about sounds plausible.

Courts are guided by rules of evidence. You won't have time to learn those rules during your divorce. But your lawyer knows them, and sometimes you're just going to have to accept the fact that certain pieces of information cannot be used in court. Often it won't seem fair and it definitely won't seem logical, at least to you, but that's the way it is. It's helpful that you understand this early on so you can prepare your case around what can and can't be used in a court of law and have realistic expectations about what the result will be.

You may believe in anything you want, including Santa Claus, but unless we're reenacting *Miracle on 34th Street,* "believing is not enough." Show us the proof.

Answering questions in depositions and at trial is completely different from chatting with friends and business associates. Be prepared to learn a new way to communicate.

Sounds easy? Think again. It's not.

How many times do we answer a question by telling an unrelated story? How many times do we answer a question with a question? How often do we guess at the answer? Just how accurate are we when asked about something that happened yesterday, the day before, last week?

Guesswork, inaccuracies, and rambling have no place in a deposition or a court of law. And if you think it's easy to break the habit of a lifetime talking that way, you may be surprised. When asked what time it is, don't explain how to make a clock.

It's necessary to be trained how to answer questions for court proceedings. Everything you say is under penalty of perjury, and once spoken, you can rarely, if ever, take back the words. You usually can correct yourself, but then you run the risk of opposing counsel's commenting on your poor memory or the very convenient revision of your testimony. Ultimately, your credibility gets called into question, and you have a new problem with which to contend.

Don't be insulted when your attorney suggests coaching you

about how to field questions. Don't get it in your head that you're an articulate, educated person and don't need any advice. *Everyone* needs help in this area.

Furthermore, your tone and mannerisms may have as much impact as your words. The testimony you give in depositions is rarely seen or heard unless the proceeding is videotaped. However, in court a judge will not only listen to what you say but observe how you say it. Let your attorney give you pointers about demeanor.

Can you recall when you were a kid and your parents said they didn't like your tone? It may still be there and slip out at the most inopportune times—such as during cross-examination by your spouse's counsel.

Be a good team player and let your attorney teach you the right way to answer questions. Your lawyer knows the ins and outs and is on home turf. You're just a player on the visiting team.

Divorce can be more time-consuming than a full-time job; be ready to devote the time needed to working with your attorney and responding to demands from the opposition.

If you think it's your lawyer who does all the work, think again. Remember finals week in high school? Well, some divorces feel exactly like the nightmare of finals week being repeated over and over again—except that your divorce may be more work.

Depending on the complexity of your case, be prepared to give a substantial amount of time to working with your attorney on the divorce. It will be necessary to meet with your lawyer; it will be necessary to prepare information and gather documents for your lawyer. It may be necessary to gather documents that have been formally demanded by the other side; it may be necessary to answer in writing numerous questions about assets, liabilities, income, and custodial arrangements. Time may be needed for your deposition to be taken, and you may need to sit in on the depositions that are being taken by your attorney. And, naturally, you may want to meet with and talk to any expert retained by you to appraise and value assets. Your lawyer needs you for all this and more.

At times you may feel as if you're going to explode. Holding down a job, trying to keep your family going, reeling from the emotional roller coaster of divorce, and then trying to find the time to take care of divorce "homework" may make you feel as though you've crossed the line into madness. Compounding the problem is the fact that meetings, depositions, and some of the preparation must be done during the daytime when you need to be at work, helping your child with her homework, or doing the laundry.

Millions have already survived this grueling experience. Start now to get in training for the masterful juggling act you're going to have to pull off. Chin up. You can do it.

Should I settle or go to court?

Tough questions and tough decisions come with the territory. Do I follow my heart or my head? Sometimes they give conflicting answers.

It's not as simple as flipping a coin. It's easier than performing brain surgery. Listen to what your advisers think. Talk to the people you trust, preferably those who don't have a stake in your decision. Sit down with your attorney and weigh the pros and cons. Give your instincts a chance to flex their muscles and do a few jumping jacks.

Then use your best judgment.

7

ARE YOU A CANDIDATE FOR MEDIATION?

We Can Work It Out

Is everyone operating in good faith? Do you trust your spouse? Is mediation for you?

Mediation is used to resolve conflicts by engaging a neutral third party to assist in the negotiation of a mutually agreeable and informed settlement. The process requires that divorcing couples have the ability to cooperate and compromise. Otherwise, it's not going to work.

Six months into the mediation, a wife was describing the assets of her business to the mediator. In the middle of her statement, her husband cried out, "You can't believe a word she says!" If that's how he felt, mediation was not a viable choice for this couple.

Picture what you will be doing. You are now going to sit down with the person with whom you once thought you would share your life. You are going to discuss dividing assets and liabilities, calculating support, sharing your children, and going your separate ways. Your spouse may have betrayed you in the "traditional" manner or in ways more subtle than a cheating spouse. Perhaps he does not have the insight or integrity or industriousness for which you once gave him credit. Perhaps she has disappointed you at home or by abandoning ideals you shared. Nonetheless, the question you must ask yourself is whether your marital partner is someone from whom you can still expect honesty and good faith at the bargaining table. If the answer is yes, you are one step closer to being a candidate for mediation.

Mediators work for the *couple*. Do you need your own advocate?

The mediator is not *your* advocate. The mediator's function it is to facilitate settlement. He or she must remain completely neutral in the process. Mediation will not be a satisfying forum if you want to get mileage from how wronged you feel. If emotions are running high, each party may be better served by having separate counsel.

If you need someone to take a strong position on your behalf and against your spouse, an advocate is a better choice than a mediator.

Mediation is not a good process for those who feel they have been victimized or abused in some fashion. Those individuals frequently have not defended themselves in the past and need someone now who is their defender rather than a neutral facilitator. If you need a Don Quixote to "right your wrongs," real or imagined, mediation is not the solution for you.

Does the size of the marital estate justify the expense of a more costly, contentious proceeding?

Although not the determining factor for or against mediation, the size of the marital estate is one factor that should be considered when examining the pros and cons of mediation.

Litigation can be a costly undertaking. Successful mediation is usually more cost effective than litigation. The size of the marital estate should be considered before plunging into litigation that may turn into an expensive battle. It is important to evaluate the benefits, risks, and costs of mediation versus retaining separate counsel and becoming part of the adversarial process.

Too often we hear stories that the cost of the divorce exceeded the size of the marital estate; the lawyers ended up with money that could have been the down payment for a new home or paid for the children's tuition. That's not to say advocates are not needed in small marital estates; often they are, because mediation is not for everyone. However, if assets are few and finances tight, it behooves both parties to consider the most efficient and economical way to resolve their differences and preserve their assets in the best way possible.

On the flip side, just because you can afford a fight doesn't necessarily mean you have to have one. If mediation is a viable alternative under your circumstances, why opt for the more costly and adversarial route?

Can you and your spouse be in the same room with a mediator and talk constructively?

It's not marriage counseling or therapy or a vehicle for catharsis; it's business. Can you do it? Many people cannot. This is something you are going to have to think about long and hard. Look inside yourself for the answer. No one can guide you better than your heart and brain. Divorce is one of the most emotional events that will ever occur in your life. Nonetheless, it's important that you enter mediation thinking more like a businessperson than a hurting spouse. If you can't, perhaps you need an advocate.

Mediation doesn't work when you or your spouse wants a forum for your anger, or revenge or to justify your conduct. It's a setting for rational, calm discussion about resolving the issues in your particular divorce. Can you talk to—not at—one another? Can you talk about the issues of the divorce rather than the issues of the marriage? Can you talk, not yell, cry, vent, emote? Because if you can't sit across from each other and talk constructively with the assistance of the mediator, then perhaps mediation is not the right choice for you.

Are there any issues in dispute about which you or your spouse will not compromise under any circumstances even if it's a deal breaker?

If that's the case, you start out with an insurmountable problem unless one of you is more flexible than you think. Just as serious a problem is the fact that this is *not* the right mind-set to have when embarking on mediation. Mediation rarely works without the spirit of compromise, something that is completely lacking if both of you are approaching a problem with your heels dug in and no room for compromise.

If there really are some points on which both of you are inflexible, you have two alternatives: forgo mediation altogether or elect to mediate specific issues and litigate others.

Will it make It easier for your children if you take the mediation route?

It may minimize the trauma for your children, but this is only one of many factors to consider when addressing the pros and cons of mediation. Naturally, any method that will result in less animosity and contentiousness between you and your spouse is better for your children. Any process that helps you best work out co-parenting issues is also a preferred approach. Your children may feel gratified knowing you are working cooperatively rather than in an adversarial setting. For some children, however, it may not make any difference. You are the best judge of your particular situation and your children.

If the marriage has one domineering partner, mediation may not be a good alternative unless the mediator prevents that person from controlling the process.

If you're married to a bully, think carefully before opting for mediation. And select a mediator very carefully if that's the route you elect to take.

Mediation sessions *cannot* consist of input, feedback, and opinions from only one partner. If that is what is going to happen, don't mediate. Those individuals who were dominated and controlled during marriage should not have to relive that experience during the divorce. *Don't make the same mistake twice.* Both of you have to give input and contribute, or mediation is pointless. If your spouse is not going to let you express yourself without interrupting, intimidating, or cutting you off, it's not going to work.

A good mediator can stop the one-sidedness that sometimes surfaces, but the mediator is not supposed to act as a cop. If he or she has to spend a considerable amount of time preventing one spouse from dominating the other and the session, you have a mediator who is not only unable to focus on the real job of dealing with your property and support issues but is also losing some of the much needed neutrality by being put in a position of warning, reprimanding, or chastising the domineering spouse. It's a cooperative process, not traffic school.

Consider the possibility of mediating one issue or isolated issues.

There can be many advantages to mediating specific issues even if the entire case can't be settled. However, don't forget: There can also be disadvantages to that solution.

Mediating a few issues can result in a tremendous cost savings. Litigation is expensive, and the fewer issues you have to try, the better off you will be.

Mediation allows more creativity than litigation. It can often produce more desirable resolutions—results that cannot be obtained in litigation. If you can obtain a preferable resolution in mediation, it's a smarter alternative. Remember that some areas of the law are black or white. Only through negotiated settlements or mediation can those gray areas be found.

It may be impossible to resolve finances with your spouse, but you can still talk civilly about the children. It is far more desirable to work out your custody and co-parenting arrangements in mediation than leaving it up to a judge. It isn't unusual for the court to come up with something that neither of you likes.

Before electing to mediate one or isolated issues, however, you should first speak with an attorney. As constructive as mediation can be, you may be doing yourself a disservice. Sometimes the issues you intend to mediate are so entwined with those you will be litigating that a mediated resolution can adversely impact the matters that will be tried by your attorney. By way of example, you may be able to resolve custody but not child support. Bear in mind that the amount of child support paid or received may be tied into the amount of time you have custody of your child. Or you may be able to resolve property division but not alimony. Don't lose sight of the fact that the amount of alimony paid or received may be affected by whether or not the spouse requesting alimony receives income-producing property.

It's a tangled web. Make sure there are no loose threads before making a final decision.

Is mediation being used by one side as a stalling tactic?

Don't be fooled. There are many reasons that people are motivated to stall, some financial, some emotional. It is critical that your motives to mediate be reasonably the same.

Be alert to the possibility that your spouse does not want the divorce or finds it difficult, if not impossible, to deal with closure. In that case, mediation may be embraced as a means for delaying the "end."

Your spouse may see this as an opportunity to keep the family together a little bit longer or a way to slow up the process. This "borrowed time" may enable your spouse to put the business or other financial affairs in as dismal and/or complicated a condition as possible in order to reduce financial exposure in the divorce. Your spouse may also see this as an opportunity to avoid or delay discovery, a more detailed investigation into the assets and liabilities of the marital estate.

A woman who had been in mediation for one year sought legal assistance because her husband still had not produced one document requested by the mediator. The woman's lawyer threatened to terminate mediation and litigate unless the husband produced every requested document immediately. The letter gave the mediation the push it needed; the husband stopped stalling, produced the requested documents, and mediation progressed.

If you know or strongly suspect that your spouse is using mediation as a stalling tactic, terminate mediation and proceed with your other options. Don't be reluctant to do what you need to do.

Whenever possible, avoid mediators with an expressed or known bias.

Mediators are supposed to be neutral, but like life, it doesn't always work out exactly as planned. Sometimes they have a bias, and sometimes a problem may exist in just your case.

Check out the reputation of your mediator. Make sure he or she doesn't already have a reputation that suggests a bias. Sometimes you'll hear that someone is "pro-wife" or "pro-husband."

A mediator should not be involved in your case if he or she has dealt with either of you before in some other capacity. It is inevitable that from the prior relationship they carry some bias or, at the very least, some preconceived ideas. This clearly creates a conflict of interest. It is not unusual for one spouse to suggest that a close personal friend, joint accountant, member of the clergy, or neighbor who happens to be an attorney act as a mediator. Watch out! The mediation is destined to fail if the mediator doesn't come to the table with complete neutrality.

It is also possible that a mediator's background or personal experiences may prejudice the mediator's approach to your case. This should be discussed as soon as discovered, and both parties and the mediator should review the advisability of proceeding with the mediation or the mediator's withdrawing.

8

ILLUSIONS AND MISCONCEPTIONS ABOUT DIVORCE

You're Nobody 'Til Somebody Loves You

The lawyers will end up with everything.
If we had a nickel for everyone who thinks this way, we wouldn't ever have to practice law again.

Lawyers have a tough reputation to live down. There's no denying that there are unscrupulous lawyers who would like to end up with all your assets, but, thankfully, they are few and far between.

Before hiring anyone, make sure you fully understand the terms of your attorney's compensation. Don't get in over your head. A person whose marital estate has a net value of $85,000 does not necessarily need an attorney who charges $375 per hour even if your best friend told you, "Hire no one else."

Most important, be sure to select an attorney whom *you* trust and respect. If you do, chances are you will be treated with the same respect, and your lawyer's goal will be to do a good job for you, not take your money.

My children will never recover from the trauma.

Your children *will* recover, although some recover faster than others. Children are far more resilient than we think. In fact, some of us could learn from them.

If children are shown love and not made to feel as if they are in the middle or part of the problem, they will heal. You can say "most children—but not my kids" all you want. Your children *will* recover, and *your* attitude toward that recovery is a critical factor in determining how long it will take.

You have lost a spouse, but your children still have two parents. Keep that in mind.

We'll be able to stay friends while we go through the divorce.

Wouldn't that be nice? Not likely, but nice.

It may be more realistic to shoot for cordial rather than friendly. Unfortunately, as you get further and further into the divorce process, you will see that staying friendly can be difficult at best. No matter how friendly the divorce, there is no denying you have conflicting goals. It is unreasonable to expect your spouse to protect you to his or her own disadvantage. In almost every case you and your spouse are adversaries at some level. While that doesn't automatically make you enemies, divorce produces conflicts of interest between your spouse and you.

A more realistic goal during the divorce is to keep it civil. If, at the conclusion, being friends is doable, then go for it.

Everything will be okay because the judge cares about me and my case.

Judges have limited time for each case and have many cases to deal with. What took you fifteen years to live through, they have to hear about, understand, and resolve in fifteen minutes. Frequently a judge cannot and does not give a case the time necessary to fully understand the rationale of your position and the ramifications of ruling one way versus another. Some judges cannot or do not find the time to read all the paperwork submitted. While judges care about fairness and the law, they are rarely more interested in your case than in the fifty other cases they must process.

After researching a point of law, we felt particularly confident about our client's position. We filed extensive declarations and briefs. When the case was called, the judge made preliminary remarks indicating we had lost. Astounded, it became evident that the judge had not read our papers. Fortunately, he suggested that he take a minute to review our papers. After he did, the result was as favorable as we had expected.

The judicial system cares about your interests only in the abstract. Judges are not your parents and do not care about how the results impact you personally. That doesn't mean judges aren't empathetic or caring. However, no judge is ever going to know you and your case as well as your lawyer does.

Judges have to follow the law, and if the law produces a result that is adverse to you, don't count on the judge overlooking the law because the result "just isn't fair" to you.

I'll never be happy again.

No better way to cheer up than a fun party. Never is a long time, and pain diminishes over time. Think of it as a beginning, and the devastation will recede. It's normal to be sad, so indulge for a while. But after being sad, look ahead.

Get on with your life. If you're feeling depressed, be receptive to whatever makes you feel better—the things that put a smile on your face. Check out the opportunities around the corner or down the hall. Don't be afraid to laugh again. It only hurts when you don't.

I'll never own a home, never be able to afford a new car, and have to work until the day I die.

All of this may be true. Or not. Everything has a tendency to look bleaker when you're in the midst of a divorce.

When the dust settles and you are ready to get on with your life, don't be surprised if your former energy and resourcefulness start inching back.

Credit can be established again so that big purchases such as cars and a home are not an impossibility. You can start building up the nest egg again if it's gone after the divorce. Sure it has the ring of starting over, but you did it before and you can do it again.

I have to stay married; my spouse will die if I leave.

It really does feel that way sometimes. It's likely that you and your spouse will both be sad if you get divorced. Your spouse may be devastated but will not die from the divorce.

If your spouse is emotionally unbalanced, it is a good idea to get him or her into counseling before breaking the news that the marriage is over. If your spouse has family members or close friends who can lend support, you might want to talk to them so that they will be prepared to help.

Some spouses will try to manipulate you into staying married by making you feel they will die without you. It may be difficult, but you have to resist the temptation to remain in the marriage out of sympathy and pity.

Be as kind as you want, but don't stay married because you think your spouse will die if you leave. It is extremely unlikely and ultimately not your responsibility. You have to do what is right for you.

The wife always gets the house and furniture; the husband always gets the business.

While this pattern was typical years ago, it is no longer the case. The law is gender neutral, and each case must be determined on its own particular facts. The court considers many factors, and there are no hard-and-fast rules. Forget the concepts that start out, "The wife *always* gets this and the husband *always* gets that."

Don't make plans based on your own assumptions. An important rule to remember is not to assume. There is no "always."

Restraining orders will prevent violence and child stealing.

A restraining order is only a piece of paper. The only thing that prevents violence and child stealing is *respect* for those orders. If you are dealing with someone who is convinced he or she is above the law or someone with no regard for the law, restraining orders are, as the saying goes, "only worth as much as the paper they're written on."

It is absolutely imperative that you take all reasonable precautions if you know you are dealing with a person who will not pay attention to restraining orders. If that is the case, it is still necessary to obtain the orders, but it's also wise not to put all your faith in the effectiveness of those orders.

Instead, find other ways to supplement the protection the orders are supposed to give you by making sure you and your children are protected from violence, including kidnapping. These methods include:

- obtaining a security system for your home;
- purchasing or renting a guard dog for protection;
- learning self defense;
- establishing signals and codes with your children;

- having neighbors and family check in regularly to make sure everything is all right;
- keeping children's passports in a safe place;
- notifying federal authorities that your children can't be removed from the country without your written consent and sending the proper authorities a copy of the court order to that effect;
- notifying schools, camps, doctors, and even the parents of your children's friends of existing restraining orders;
- always knowing where your children are supposed to be, including phone numbers and addresses;
- avoiding isolated places, particularly at night.

There are no guarantees. The bottom line is that common sense, good luck, *and* restraining orders combined will go a long way to protect you and your children. If you're dealing with a threat, always be on the alert and assume the worst.

A mother always gets custody of the children. No judge will give a father custody.

Welcome to a new era. Courts look at what arrangement is in the best interests of children, and that means abandoning the stereotypical knee-jerk reaction of the past that children always live with their mothers.

Many people are able to work out a custody agreement. In the absence of an agreement, the court awards custody to the parent who is better able to meet the best interests of the children. A mother does not automatically get custody. A father can get custody if he is the better parent. Alternatively, the parties may end up with a shared custodial arrangement.

Any legitimate request for custody will be treated seriously by the court. This does not include requests that are designed to "get even" with the other parent, efforts to thwart the other parent's contact with the children, or strategies to receive more or pay less child support.

The best plan is the one that best suits the needs of your particular child.

The husband always pays for the wife's attorney's fees.

Guess again. There are very few "always" in divorce, and this isn't one of them.

There are many sources from which your attorney's fees may be paid. The circumstances of your case will dictate the ultimate source. In most states the party with the ability to pay is the one who pays. Sometimes each party bears his or her own fees and costs, or most of them. The fees for both or one party may be paid from funds accumulated during the marriage. The source of payment is not automatic, and even in the case of a working husband and nonworking wife, there is no assurance that the husband will have to pay his wife's fees.

Courts look at many factors, including the needs of the parties and their respective ability to pay their own and the other party's fees. The court may also look at the conduct of the parties during the case.

Make sure you have the resources to pay your attorney because the court may decide that is your responsibility.

Marriage doesn't work; I'll never get married again.

Never is a long time. You'll go through more changes than the weather. Divorce is a time when we talk with the heart and not with the head.

Remarriage is the triumph of hope over experience. Thank goodness for that. Throughout his divorce, a friend kept saying he'd never get remarried. About one year after the divorce he married his divorce lawyer. Invariably the ones who make this vow of monogamy the loudest and longest are the first ones down the aisle after the divorce is over. You say, "Never again, not me," and our response is, "Will we be getting an invitation to the wedding?"

Your spouse won't use your secrets or weaknesses against you.

In a perfect world, you could count on that. But it's not perfect, so prepare yourself.

When your vulnerabilities are exposed, the reaction ranges from heartbreak to rage. Apoplexy may strike when you read a declaration filled with confidences spilled out during more trusting times. But it happens a lot. You can't stop your spouse. The best way you can protect yourself is by being psychologically prepared for the treacherous outpourings and ready to present whatever information you have to counteract those disclosures. If your spouse attempts to use your weaknesses against you, be ready. If your spouse is a better negotiator, don't negotiate. Leave that to your attorney. If your spouse gets to you with tears, don't meet privately. Use common sense to take care of yourself.

Do not lose sight of the old adage "All's fair in love and war," and don't forget that divorce can be war.

You feel guilty about ending the marriage and believe you should give more and get less.

Guilt is a strong emotion and not a rational motivation for any action. It doesn't belong in a business deal. Dividing your property is a business deal, and you must be fair to everyone, including yourself. There is no problem with being generous. In fact, being generous may produce long-term benefits that are hard to anticipate. However, "giving away the store" because of guilt is not generosity and often is not appreciated. You may kick yourself in a few years and come to resent what you gave up. Make sure the deal you strike is one you can accept as circumstances change in the future.

The best advice we've given clients who remain determined, because of guilt, to pay more than they should is to enter into an agreement that is fair now, set the "guilt" money aside, and wait for a substantial period of time after the divorce is over to see if they still feel the same way. If the urge remains, follow through with the impulse. No doubt your generosity won't be refused.

My spouse is doing everything possible to make me suffer.

It may feel that way, but more often than not that's not the case. Divorce is a time when each person stops thinking in terms of "us" and starts thinking in terms of "me." It's not so much that your spouse wants you to suffer. It's that your spouse now wants what only she or he desires and is no longer taking your needs and desires into consideration. Now "it's every man for himself."

Life will never be normal again.

It all depends on how one defines "normal." Life is going to be different. Different can be good or bad depending on what you make of it.

You will establish new routines and make new friends. After the stress and interference of litigation is reduced, you'll be surprised how fast your life returns to comfortable patterns.

It's a new beginning, and you'll redefine what is now normal in your life. Don't be hung up on doing everything the way you did it before and parroting the past.

Once the divorce is over, it's over.

Sometimes, but often not. Ouch! Many court orders are modifiable, and, accordingly, a final judgment lacks the finality it boasts.

Usually child and spousal support as well as child custody can be changed. You can be looking at the inside of a courthouse again after the divorce is over.

Proceedings to enforce existing orders can also reactivate the case.

On a less literal level, those parties who have children will continue to deal with one another for many years to come. At times those contacts may make you feel as if the divorce, or even the marriage, never ended.

Even for those who do not have children, it is important to be prepared for the reality that you still may be dealing with your former spouse on issues left over from the marriage. A few common examples are:

- an audit of a joint income tax return;
- sale of real property and other assets;
- the division of retirement plans.

The one part of divorce that's truly "over when it's over" is that you're no longer married. Just make sure your final decree or judgment is actually processed by the court and you have a copy of that document with the official court filing stamp on it! Once you have the "final," you can have your divorce party or remarry—or both.

9

TEMPER, TEMPER

Don't Be Cruel

That feeling that you want to kill your spouse? Channel it elsewhere.

Did you ever feel so angry you thought you could kill someone? Most of us have. Hang in there. Let it pass or find a constructive outlet.

Feelings are in our heads and hearts, and if not expressed by words or conduct, no one is damaged and no one is the wiser. If bottling up these feelings causes you trouble, get professional help.

Control yourself. Do not destroy property.

This is not the time to indulge in the philosophy "If it feels good, do it!" Do not steal, destroy, tear, cut, saw, or damage something special to your spouse—or anything, for that matter. Nor should you put your fist through the wall, the mirror, or anything else. The only list longer than the list of what you shouldn't do is the list of repercussions you can expect from those actions. The price you pay can be as mild as a miffed spouse or as unpleasant as jail time.

If you don't want to pay your spouse top dollar for that ugly lamp you always hated, don't smash it. Control yourself! You'll be way ahead in the long run if you can look at the big picture and not let your anger be your master. Here's one guy who didn't look at the big picture: After an argument with his wife about an expensive and prized work of art, in a fit of rage the husband sliced the painting in half with a kitchen knife, while screaming, "Now we can both have it!"

As tempting as destruction may seem, don't do it. There are many reasons to hold back, not the least of which are restraining orders prohibiting such conduct. If you can think of no other good reason, use that one. Unlike your mother, the law is not forgiving if your temper gets out of hand.

This type of behavior has ramifications that may be far reaching and devastating. Losing credibility. Affecting custody. Hurting you financially. Incurring civil and criminal consequences.

In other words, a five-second temper tantrum can ruin your life.

You can't unring the bell. Watch what you say in anger, confusion, and grief.

Remember that in this day and age of videotaping, voice mail, e-mail, and answering machines, your words can be preserved forever and come back to haunt you.

You know that old expression "hoisted on your own petard"? Well, don't let that be you. Don't blurt out your lawyer's strategy. Anything said or written by you to your spouse can be used to your detriment and will invariably show up later in some court document or testimony.

In your marital litigation, virtually everything you say or write can be repeated. If you don't want to hear it again in court, restrain yourself. Nothing is more embarrassing than being in court and listening to a tape of yourself cursing and screaming like a maniac, at the same time that you're trying to convince the judge you are a reasonable, fair-minded person who always treated your spouse with respect.

Before giving your spouse anything you've written, pretend that the judge assigned to your case will be reading it. If it can pass that test, the tone and content are probably okay. If not, don't send it.

The most prejudicial evidence the other side can produce is your own statement, especially when your words are memorialized in writing or on tape. This evidence can't be challenged. In one matter a husband came through the door swinging and screaming obscenities and threats as his wife was leaving a voice mail message for her friend. At a subsequent hearing the husband denied the whole incident. The wife played the tape recording of her husband's words which had been memorialized forever on her friend's answering machine.

Those of you with children should also remember that your children may play back the answering machine, read e-mail messages, or find letters from you to your spouse. Your children may be scared, disturbed, or confused by the content and the tone of the messages from you when you don't use good judgment.

You will protect yourself and save money in the long run if you check with your lawyer *before* you send a letter. It's a sensible precaution that will save you the expense and grief of having your lawyer do damage control later.

Don't talk to your spouse if you can't control your temper or if your spouse is an expert at pushing your buttons. If you find yourself losing your cool, count to ten, twenty, one hundred, whatever it takes to cool down. Write the letter and rip it up. Talk to your mirror. Take a cold shower. Don't look to confront your spouse when you're angry about something. Wait one, two, three days. Whatever works. Skip the conversation with your spouse and let communications be done through the attorneys.

Never hit, push, shove, strike, or attack your spouse.

Ever seen the inside of a jail anywhere other than on TV or in the movies? Well, you may if you decide to resort to violence. And don't think that violence means the kind you see in the Dirty Harry movies. Assaults include scratching, shoving, biting, slapping, punching, pinching, and nonconsensual sexual attacks. Initiating any kind of physical assault or altercation against your spouse will be more than enough for you to be given time to think about your conduct in a jail cell. No one is exempt.

This is not a joking matter. Under absolutely no circumstances should you physically assault your spouse unless you are defending yourself from assault. Even then the best alternative is to make a hasty exit rather than defend.

An assault can spiral your case right into criminal court. Not only are these acts criminal, but they can be dangerous to you if your spouse retaliates. Needless to say, the repercussions in your divorce case will invariably be nothing short of disastrous. There are no circumstances under which this type of behavior will be sanctioned by the court.

Take a deep breath and control your urge to strike out. This is one of those times when you must keep your temper. You have a lot more to lose than money.

Separation is not the time to tell your spouse about every single incident you resented during the marriage and every little thing you don't like about him or her.

If your fuse is short or your self-discipline is minimal, do yourself a favor and either refrain from talking to your spouse altogether or map out everything you are going to say in advance.

Separation may feel like the opportune moment to let your spouse "have it." Perhaps you've been saving up and working on the exact words that will reduce your spouse to tears. If that's the case, just keep it to yourself. You may find your revenge backfires, and in the end it doesn't help you, so why do it? If you just can't keep your feelings bottled up, by all means go to a therapist or a trustworthy friend and let loose. You may feel better, and you won't run the risk of making your spouse an enemy or devastating someone you once loved.

Since you are no longer trying to save the marriage, what can be gained other than a momentary smirk of satisfaction? Balance that against what you have to lose, and the smart money says to keep your temper in check and your mouth zipped.

Don't harass your spouse—no stalking or annoying phone calls.

Just leave your spouse alone. Move on, get a life, and if you can't, see a therapist or leave town for a while. Harassment can have civil, criminal, and financial ramifications. You don't need this on top of everything else. This behavior has no upside. Eventually it will impact the world outside your divorce, including your relationship with friends and your employment. No one wants a "kook" around, and it's hard to characterize this type of conduct as anything else.

No one other than another kook will be on your side. Your spouse will garner support and sympathy, hardly the goal you were going for.

You're wrong if you think no one will be able to prove it's you doing these things. The spouse is always the number one suspect.

Have a cooling-off period; decisions made in anger are often regretted later.

Divorce is a time of high emotions. If you can avoid making spur-of-the-moment decisions, you will be well ahead of the game. Those decisions are often nothing more than knee-jerk reactions. Your divorce will impact your future, so careful consideration is hardly a waste of time. A decision made while hotheaded should not control the course of your life, but it can.

This advice applies not only to decisions about getting a divorce, moving out, and selling the house but also to settlement proposals. Sometimes you are so angry at your spouse, that you may turn down an advantageous settlement proposal. Don't be your own worst enemy.

Before he retained us, one client called his wife and told her, "I'll accept your settlement proposal. Have your attorney draw up the papers. Just go away and leave me alone." The wife was angry and refused to accept her own proposal, saying, "He can't tell me what to do." What a mistake! When the case was tried, the wife received less than half of what she had originally requested.

Make your decisions when you're calm and rational. Be prepared to consider and accept the long-term consequences of what you decide.

Try different methods to cope with your temper.

Hitting your head against the wall is definitely not one of the better solutions, so try different methods to cope with anger: Read books on the subject, consult with a professional, meditate. Different things work for different people.

If you've identified yourself as an individual with a hair-trigger temper, then identify the best method to help you get it under control.

Your anger is your enemy in a divorce. If you can't effectively cope with it, get help. Therapists are a good source of assistance with anger. Find one who is willing to help you with only this issue if that's all you want addressed. Reading books on the subject may sound a little lame, but don't knock it until you've tried it. On your own, in conjunction with other methods, take time to seek out things that soothe you. Golf. Listen to music. Paint. Do physical exercise. Walk in a park. Go to the library. Watch old comedies. You may just need a punching bag.

You'll find that controlling your anger will have benefits way beyond your divorce.

Count to ten before rejecting a proposal made by your spouse.

Sometimes it's not that we say no but how we say it. Give yourself time to think before responding. After all, you never know when you may be making a proposal to your spouse.

People who are alienated from each other do not believe that the other person has anything valuable or rational to say. Before you simply reject a proposal, however, analyze it. See if there's any basis for settlement. See if you can detect what's really important to your spouse so that you can be a better negotiator. If you have any question or hesitation, you should consult your attorney; he or she will be more objective and has more experience. You're paying the lawyer for advice—listen to it.

Don't lose your temper in court, during your deposition, or in psychological evaluations.

You say it'll never happen. "I wouldn't be dumb enough to lose my temper in court or at an evaluation." Wanna bet? A lot of people have said just that and then exploded on the witness stand.

Don't ask us how it happens. Don't ask us how intelligent

people can blow it that way. They do. Temper comes from a different source than our logical and rational thought process.

If you have a bad temper, you lose it at the worst possible times. If you know you have this problem, it's critical to work on controlling your anger. Needless to say, such control can ultimately make or break your case.

Frequently, in divorce cases, you are judged by how you behave in stressful situations. Those situations, however, usually last only a brief period of time. Remember, no matter how justifiable your anger is, you're the one who loses if you lose your cool. Just take a deep mental breath and keep your temper. It just may be that the attorney who represents your spouse is trying to get you to blow up; you're playing right into the attorney's hands if you lose your temper. So if your spouse's attorney needles you, just ignore it. Give a sincere answer, and you'll retain the upper hand.

Do not send anonymous letters or make anonymous phone calls to friends, employers, relatives, parents, or lovers of your spouse.

You may think you're very clever, but it's not always that difficult to figure out the source. Are you up for the war of attrition? What if *your* friends, employers, relatives, parents, and lovers start receiving anonymous letters or phone calls?

You'd be surprised how many people get caught doing this, particularly in this age when the telephone company offers caller ID as well as instant callback. You may be in for an unpleasant shock—finding out that the person you called knows just who you are.

These tactics are not constructive. You may end up making innocent people suffer, for example, if you leave a message meant for one relative and another one gets it.

If you have an irresistible impulse to communicate, write a letter but tear it up immediately without keeping copies that may fall into the wrong hands.

Don't forget that harassing letters and calls (even anonymous) are in violation of restraining orders, and there are punishments if you get caught. It's just not worth it.

Do not obsess about small issues. Try to stay patient, flexible, and understanding when dealing with your spouse.

In the divorce process there may be relatively minor points of contention that you should ignore. "It isn't fair." That is frequently true, but no one, including your attorney, wants you to run up a $10,000 bill over a $200 clock.

If you're near settlement, this is not the time for either side to say "no deal" when, for example,

- your spouse insists that she be awarded the lawnmower;
- your spouse insists that he have custody of the children for Thanksgiving in even years instead of odd years;
- a disagreement arises about payments being one-half on the first and one-half on the fifteenth of the month, or the fifth and twentieth of the month;
- your spouse insists on keeping the turtle;
- your spouse forgets that you don't take cream with your coffee; it's his new significant other who does;
- your spouse gave away the Lakers basketball tickets and forgot that she promised them to you.

Move on. Concentrate on the big issues. Try to keep things in perspective. The more flexible you can be, the better chance you have to settle your case. And settlement is almost always better than trial. It is usually less expensive, and each of you is likely to get more satisfaction. Understanding your spouse is crucial.

Litigate what you absolutely can't resolve. Narrow the issues. And try to see things a little bit from your spouse's point of view. It takes two to get married, and it takes two to settle. You'll end up saving yourself money and heartache.

10

THE PROS AND CONS
OF THERAPY

Lean on Me

Thinking they know what they're doing when they don't, many therapists give legal advice.

Your therapist is *not* your lawyer. If a therapist is foolish enough to give legal advice, don't be foolish enough to take it.

Some therapists give advice that is contrary to their patient's best legal and financial interests.

This happens frequently and can lead to unfortunate results. This story is amazing. Five years after their marriage, a woman with substantial assets presented her husband with a postnuptial agreement. The husband consulted an attorney, who advised him not to sign the agreement. At their next joint therapy session, the husband asked their therapist for a recommendation. The therapist voiced an opinion that it would be great for their marriage if the husband signed. So he did. Unfortunately for the husband, when the couple divorced, he discovered that signing the agreement had been about the worst thing he could ever have done.

Any advice that touches on the legal and financial aspects of your life should be reviewed by your lawyer before you act on it.

Therapists often give you a perspective that enables you to cope better with the pain and trauma of divorce.

It's vital to recognize if you need therapy. Not everyone going through a divorce needs help, but a lot of us do. Some people are so overwhelmed by the pain and so confused by the change that the ability to think clearly is lost. For others the anger can be overpowering. There is nothing embarrassing or wrong about acknowledging that you can't "get through it" alone. Therapists can help put things in perspective and make the transition easier from the old lifestyle to a new one.

Custody solutions from therapists can be toxic.

Although a therapist's advice on your custody problems may be well meaning, the legal ramifications can be unanticipated and hard to reverse. While it may seem wise to allow the children to flow back and forth between their parents, the decision to just "try this out and see how it works" can be disastrous because it sets a precedent. Consult with your attorney before you start implementing a schedule that can take on a life of its own.

Oblivious to the financial strain it may cause, therapists may encourage you to beg, borrow, and "steal" in order to continue in therapy with them.

Usually there are competent professionals to be found at an affordable price. Many therapists will work within your budget; others have sliding scales. If your therapist is unable to accommodate your financial circumstances, you have to consider finding someone else. Most important, your therapist is not there to *add* to your pressures.

Confidentiality may disappear when a therapist sees both you and your spouse. Be cautious about what you say in joint sessions.

Having your own words—uttered in what you thought was a private, heart-wrenching moment—thrown back in your face in a court of law can be devastating.

A husband's confession in joint therapy that he had a substance abuse problem came as a complete shock to his wife. While the therapist's testimony regarding the session might not be admissible, the wife was now armed with the information she needed to win the custody battle. She informed the court that her husband had a substance abuse problem. The court ordered drug testing, which revealed that the husband had been telling the truth.

While your therapist is encouraging you and your spouse to "tell all," it's essential to keep in mind the possibility that things may deteriorate in the future and your spouse may want to use your "tell-all" to your disadvantage.

Therapists can facilitate your family's transition, help in the resolution of family problems, and make you a better parent.

You have a big problem on your hands. You are trying to keep your family happy and stable while going through one of the unhappiest and least stable times of your life. Therapists see families in this kind of turmoil and often have good ideas and helpful input to make this difficult time easier.

Sometimes it's hard to see the forest for the trees. Be open to ideas and approaches you may not have considered. Our client and his wife were unable to agree on how to divide some money. The husband claimed it was his; the wife claimed it was hers. The conflict was beginning to turn a peaceful divorce into an ugly mess. Both parties were thrilled with the therapist's suggestion that they put all the disputed money in a trust for their children.

It may be helpful for your children to talk with someone individually or in a family session or both. A therapist may have pointers that enable you to do a better job. It never hurts to listen.

When considering whether you or your family needs a therapist, ask yourself some questions. Are you and your children communicating effectively? Are you coping with your parenting responsibilities? Are any of your children acting out or having special problems as a result of the divorce? Are you or the children acting abusively? Have unhealthy patterns or behavior changes taken place?

If you find there are too many questions that have a yes answer, consider the advantages of therapy for you and your children.

Therapists with their own closure problems will not cut you loose even if there is no longer a need for therapy.

The goal of therapy is to face and deal with your difficult issues, not create new ones. Don't become dependent on your therapist. If you've accomplished as much as you can in therapy, make the break and end the sessions. Therapists should assist you in doing this, but sometimes they don't. Talk to your therapist if you think the time has come to wind down or terminate sessions. See if he or she agrees with you. Listen closely to your therapist's reasoning for continuing with sessions. If it makes sense, perhaps you should continue. If it doesn't, perhaps the problem lies with the therapist and not you.

Do not transfer the responsibility for your decisions from your spouse to your therapist.

Your therapist is not a substitute for your spouse; don't replace one dependency with another. Your goal is to be a self-sufficient individual. This does not mean that you shouldn't have a new mate or a therapist. It does mean, however, that you're going to have to accept responsibility for your life and decisions. If you allowed your former spouse to make your decisions, don't compound that error by trying to get your therapist to be your new decision-maker.

It's wise to have an objective person to consult while you're going through a difficult divorce. A therapist can be a lot less expensive and more "therapeutic" than your lawyer.

Sometimes it's easier to talk to a stranger than to a friend. If you need to vent or cry or embark on a catharsis that may take who knows how long, or just talk about what's going on, it's often a better idea to find a good therapist than use your lawyer. Your lawyer may be a tempting candidate. Who knows better what you are going through? Using your lawyer, however, is too expensive and not nearly as productive as using a therapist. A therapist will not only listen and understand but may give you insights you lack and useful input for the future.

Taking a drug prescribed by your therapist may adversely impact you in a divorce proceeding.

Certain therapists are enthusiastic about having their patients take prescription drugs, but the legality of prescription drugs, especially those for psychological conditions, does not necessarily mean it is accepted by society or by the legal process. Particularly in custody cases, the use of prescription drugs often becomes the catalyst for allegations of unfitness or worse. Accusations of addiction will not be ignored even though the drug is prescribed. Before taking or even filling a prescription for drugs, it's a good idea to talk to your attorney and find out if such action will impact your case.

Select your therapist with the same amount of care and attention that you would any other professional.

Don't choose a therapist solely because someone "loved" him or her, or you like the convenience of the office location. The decision about a therapist should be made as carefully as the selection of your attorney. Get recommendations from sources you trust, such as your family doctor, clergy, attorney, school counseling centers, community mental health agencies, friends, family service centers, other therapists, and hospital outpatient clinics.

Arrange some initial interviews and be prepared to ask the questions that are important to you. Find out if the therapist has any type of bias, such as gender, religious, philosophical, or lifestyle. Consider whether this person is someone with whom you could open up comfortably. Do you like the therapist's demeanor, attitude, sense of humor? Some of it is just instinct. If you have done your homework in advance to ensure the level of professional competence, it's usually okay to trust your instincts.

If you are not the "type" for therapy but could use a support system, consider some alternatives.

In some communities, having a therapist is as routine as getting up in the morning and taking a shower, but for some people it still has a stigma. Therapy is not for everyone, but that doesn't mean you have to go through the ordeal of divorce completely alone. There are different types of support groups. One of them might be just the right fit for you.

In regional newspapers and the free weekly throwaways that circulate in many cities and counties, there are ads for women's and men's organizations, for people who are single, widowed, divorced, or part of a co-dependent relationship. The options are virtually unlimited. You can ask your attorney, clergy, and local hospitals about groups. If you don't want to ask a particular person, look into your community's groups for single and divorced people, therapy groups sponsored by individual therapists, mental health clinics and hospitals, Parents Without Partners organizations, consciousness-raising groups, and other similar sources.

Not all groups are what they advertise. But if you find one that suits you, give it a chance. Help in whatever form it comes should always be welcome.

11

PROTECTING YOUR CHILDREN

Mamas, Don't Let Your Babies
Grow Up to Be Cowboys

Reassure your children that the divorce is not about them and that both parents love them very much.

Children often think the divorce is their fault. They feel responsible and guilty. Your children need to know the divorce is between their parents. They need reassurance that they are loved by both parents, even if Mom and Dad no longer want to live together.

How will I pay for tutors, private school, and college for my kids?

It would give you immeasurable relief if we could respond to this by saying, "No problem." But, unfortunately, that's not the case. Whether or not you can afford tutors, private school, and college tuition is almost completely dependent on the economic situation when the dust settles and the divorce is concluded.

Few states have laws that would require either spouse to pay for college education; this is considered a voluntary act. The first question is whether you or your spouse is agreeable to accepting this responsibility. The second question, of course, even if you or your ex is agreeable, is whether you can afford to do it. If this is a priority and you are concerned that you won't have the money to send your children to college, try to talk to your former spouse about setting up a college fund to which each of you makes a contribution monthly or annually. Be sure the money is earmarked for your children's college education and cannot be used or withdrawn for any other purpose. It would be best to have an attorney draw up an agreement or order memorializing this arrangement.

The bottom line is, unless there is an agreement or order requiring one or both parents to pay, the best plan is to assume you have full responsibility for the financial obligation and start saving for it today.

If finances are tight, put yourself on a regular schedule of making contributions to a savings plan for your children's education. If you deposit $25 a week into a savings account, you will have over $5,000 at the end of four years. It's never too late to start, but the sooner you start, the better.

The issue of payment for tutors and private school is a little different. This can be addressed by your attorney in connection with negotiating your divorce. Be sure to let your lawyer know these issues exist and that you would like to have your spouse pay or contribute to these expenses. Depending on your respective incomes and the assets of your marriage, it is possible the judgment can address responsibility for payment of these expenses. However, if there isn't enough money to go around, private school may not be an affordable option.

With respect to both college and private school, be sure to look into all the available options for reduced tuition, which includes those based on need, financial aid, and scholarships.

If there are continuing custody issues, keep records of all events involving your children.

You may think you'll never forget disturbing incidents until the day you die, but trust us, under tough cross examination you may find you have forgotten just enough to undermine your credibility.

If there are continuing custody issues, we strongly recommend that you keep a journal chronicling anything of importance that is relevant to the children and any dispute you are having with their other parent. Note the date, time, place, and witnesses to any conversation, event, altercation, or even observation you may later need to bring to the court's attention. The more detailed your records, the better. The list of things you should chronicle could go on forever, but by way of example, here are a few events you will need to be able to relate to the court with as much detail as possible:

- conversations on the phone or in person in which your former spouse has been uncooperative about giving you information about the children's health, progress at school, after-school activities, or any other matters of importance relating to your children;
- any incidents in which your former spouse has attempted to obstruct or thwart your custodial time with your children;
- any complaints your children have related to you about verbal or physical abuse by their other parent or while in the other parent's custody;
- your children returning from your former spouse with bruises, ill, or looking dirty, unkempt, and neglected;
- your children relating things they have heard or witnessed while with your former spouse which you consider inappropriate or dangerous;
- observations of your spouse drinking or using drugs while caring for the children;
- a decline in your child's grades or conduct marks. Keep

copies of these school reports if you are the non-custodial parent.

Write down the actual words spoken to you or the exchange between you and your spouse. Memories fade, conversations start to blend into one another, and months later it's difficult to remember the things said by everyone at a particular time and place. Write down as much as you can. It's better to err on the side of caution. This type of "journal" can be extremely useful later when preparing declarations for court or testifying. They can be referred to in order to refresh your recollection and give the most accurate account of what occurred, when it happened, and who witnessed the events. If you have this journal, it may also be used to refresh the recollection of your witnesses.

When traumatic events occur, we may think they are burned into our memory. The truth is that the more upsetting the incident, the more likely our recollection of it will get hazy as time passes.

What do I do if my ex is verbally or physically abusing the children? Do I report every incident? Should I embellish or manufacture events?

Really listen to what your children tell you. Hear what they're saying and not saying. Not all child abuse is easily observed. Be aware and sensitive if your child is trying to tell you about a problem with your former spouse or your significant other. *Listen to your children.* Evidence of abuse can surface in more subtle ways. Nightmares, crying jags for no apparent reason, sensitivity to certain topics, seemingly irrational fears, or coming home with bruises. Or your child may tell you about excessive yelling or grossly unsuitable methods of punishment and discipline.

If there is abuse, it *must* be reported. Call the police or the Department of Social Services immediately and tell your attorney at once so that appropriate restraining orders and/or modifications to the custody arrangement can be obtained right away.

Every county has agencies that should be notified. Your attorney or the children's physician can direct you to the appropriate agency. If there is evidence of any physical abuse, your child should immediately be taken to a doctor. The doctor will care for your child and will also serve as independent verification of your child's condition for the court and any investigation.

Under no circumstances should you lie, embellish, or exaggerate. If you suspect abuse but don't think you have enough evidence, *do not* concoct a story in an effort to accomplish something you feel you may not otherwise obtain. *Do not* exaggerate appropriate discipline your spouse has imposed on your child and transform it into some kind of abuse. The ramifications of this type of conduct by you can be far-reaching and devastating.

In a particularly disturbing case, a mother arbitrarily decided she wanted the father to spend less time with their boys. To accomplish this goal, she took pictures of severe black and blue marks on one of the boy's legs. Then she called the county department in charge of children's welfare, alleged that the father was beating the boys, and showed them the pictures. The county department recommended that the children remain with her pending further investigation. Without giving the father notice, and based on the written recommendation of the county, the mother obtained a court order prohibiting the father from having any contact with the children. He was shocked, confused, and devastated, and retained us to get his children back. When the children were questioned at the court's direction, without the mother being present, both children independently confirmed that their mother knew the bruises were actually from falling off a bicycle. The children were adamant that their father did not beat them or cause the bruises. The court was appalled with the mother's deception, and she lost custody of the children.

If you don't like the way your spouse interacts, disciplines, or speaks to your child, there are ways to bring this to the court's attention and make changes. What constitutes verbal abuse is subject to interpretation. If you have evidence that your child is the subject of verbal abuse, seek court orders restraining the abuse or other orders modifying custody to prevent the abuse from continuing. But be careful: Just because your child alleges something is happening doesn't necessarily mean it is.

Try to keep the children's day-to-day schedule and environment consistent with their pre-separation agenda.

Children are perceptive and sensitive, and you can't pretend things haven't changed. Try to make changes in the other aspects of their lives as minimal as possible.

Obviously you can't hide the fact that you and your spouse no longer live together. Children are usually unhappy about this change in their lives and will ask a lot of questions. Try to make everything else stay as routine as possible because this will increase their feeling of security.

Keep the same meal schedule and homework and play schedules. Try to let your children see their friends as often as before. Let them see that life will go on in the pattern and flow to which they have become accustomed. Allow them to take clothes and toys back and forth between the two households as they please. Be sure both you and your spouse coordinate and know the children's schedules so that they don't miss parties, team practices and games, school events, and things of this nature. Inform each other of scheduled plans and events; it will provide your children with a port in the storm of divorce.

Don't argue with your spouse or put your spouse down in front of the children.

You may no longer love, honor, or respect your spouse, but your children should. Your spouse is still a parent, and you gain nothing and lose a lot by doing anything that hurts your child's relationship with your spouse. The marriage may be over, but children still do better knowing they have two parents who love them and on whom they can rely.

By demeaning your spouse in front of your children, by arguing with your spouse and letting your children see animosity and anger, you run the risk that your children will feel they should mimic your behavior. They may think that what you say and feel about their parent is right and that they, too, should be or can be hostile and disrespectful to your spouse.

There is also another possibility. Children often rally to protect a parent who is being attacked. If you continually fight with your spouse in front of your child and put your spouse down, you may find that your child will defend and protect your spouse and "parent" that spouse in a role reversal.

The bottom line is that children should not be subjected to this type of conduct. It's hurtful and damaging because it puts them in a conflict between two people they love. Moreover, you become a poor role model. You are the person from whom your children learn. Conduct yourself in a manner that you would be proud to have them imitate.

Make sure that the temporary and permanent orders contain provisions that allocate responsibility for the payment of doctors, dentists, and psychologists for your children.

If a medical crisis strikes, the last thing you want to be concerned about is the ability to pay for necessary care and treatment for your child. But problems can arise if the necessary provisions have not been included in your orders.

It is essential that your temporary and permanent orders set forth who will pay for medical and hospitalization coverage for your children and how uninsured expenses will be paid. Frequently settlements include provisions preventing large uninsured or unreimbursed expenses to be incurred without mutual agreement. It is also not unusual to require both parties to consent before children undergo psychological or psychiatric treatment. But every case is different.

When medical and dental insurance are financially possible, they are the best solution. If not, a court order requiring your spouse to pay all or half of these expenses will help. If there is no help in sight and you are on your own, try to put money away regularly to save for these inevitable expenses.

If your child has special medical problems or circumstances, your agreement should address how the payment for that medical care will be handled.

Therapy may be desirable, but it is rarely a necessity. If you've decided your child would benefit from therapy, contact the therapist and see what financial alternatives are available. Some therapists accept credit cards; others have payment plans. Many clinics have "sliding" payment scales that allow you to pay in accordance with your ability.

The more detailed the terms of your agreement, the less stress you will have later in dealing with the payment of your child's medical expenses, and the more attention you can give your sick child.

How do I introduce the new person in my life to my children?

Very carefully. It's different for every family. The important thing is for you to recognize that you can't just drop this person into your child's world. You need to give some thought to this transition.

Your child's reaction to a new person can run the gamut from enthusiasm to hostility. Even if your child already knows and likes the person, liking a person as a teacher, coach, or parent of a friend is not the same as having that person thrust into your personal life. Try to find a comfortable and non-threatening way to introduce your new person to your child. Before you introduce the new person, think about when the time is right, what sort of plans are appropriate, and what your children's reactions will be. The goal is for them to be comrades, not competitors. Be sure your child knows that nothing and no one will ever change how much you love your child.

Visitation arrangements should be made between you and your spouse; do not put the children in the middle of the conflict or make them feel the decision is theirs.

When working out visitation arrangements, it's usually a bad, and often a terrible, idea to tell children, "It's up to you. What do you want?" They're still your children; you and your spouse are still the grown-ups, although you both may not always act like it. Decisions concerning visitation should be made between you and your spouse. Your children should *not* be involved.

When you give your children the authority to decide with which parent they spend time, they will come up with manipulative strategies. Children often play one parent off against the other. It's not unusual for them to see from which feuding parent they can get more gifts, freedom, or any other perk.

Although your children need to understand what's happening, try to shelter them from the fallout from the divorce as much as possible. Putting them in the middle of the conflict will potentially scar and traumatize them. They will feel more secure when you set reasonable limits and maintain the role of the parent.

How do I face my former spouse when we attend events involving our children? How do we avoid awkward situations?

If you and your former spouse were getting along well, you wouldn't be asking this question.

The way you act when you see your former spouse, particularly when your children are present and especially at events involving your children, should be civil—defined as courteous and polite. If that's not possible, just avoid each other. If you feel up to the part, try cordial, which is a little bit warmer. You don't need to be outgoing, friendly, and effusive. You don't have to chat up a storm, but you owe it to your children to be civil. So do it whether you like it or not, whether it's sincere or not. Glaring at the other person, sniggering behind your hand, and making derogatory comments are guaranteed to make it awkward and uncomfortable for your children. Try to remember that you were once close to your children's other parent.

It may be an effort, but think of it as your shot at an Academy Award.

Try to figure out what's best for your child.

Think about your child first, not yourself. If your child wants to go with your spouse during your custodial time, don't be consumed with guarding "your" time. It's Saturday night, your ex has two tickets to the all-star game, and your child is dying to go. But it's your weekend, and you've been looking forward to spending that time with your child. This is the time to put your child first. Then the star who really shines is you.

Sometimes you'll have to postpone your Sunday golf game because miniature golf is more appropriate for your five-year-old.

Get the point?

Over and over again you'll find yourself facing the prospect of balancing your ego, weighing your needs against the demands of your child, and determining what is best for your child. With or without divorce, it's a problem all parents face. During a divorce this conflict becomes particularly difficult because there's an even greater desire to prove that you're a "super" parent. You want to show that your child is doing great notwithstanding the difficult times. The temptation is to show you're the better, more caring parent, but it's not a competition with your former spouse.

Keep your objectives in perspective and do what's best for your child.

Do I have to invite my ex if I'm throwing a party for our child? Should I consider what our child wants?

What do you think? Really, only you know the right answer, and it depends on your particular circumstances. No, you don't have to invite your ex to the party you are throwing. With that answer out of the way, you now have to explore what you should do, which may be entirely different.

Failing to consider what your child wants may boomerang. The party is not for you but for your child. If your child adamantly wants your ex to be there, should you put your problems with your ex ahead of that consideration? Under some extreme circumstances the answer may be yes. Otherwise, think long and hard about what you are taking away from your child's special day by not inviting your ex.

If the decision is made and you are reluctantly including your former spouse, you may want to call ahead of time and discuss some ideas for ensuring that the day goes peacefully.

However, if you and your ex can't be in the same room without unpleasantness, unless an order or agreement requires you to include him or her, don't send that invitation.

Should my child have a separate telephone number so that calls with the other parent don't involve me?

The answer to this question requires consideration of many factors, including your child's age and maturity level, how aggravated you are by having to tell your child the other parent is on the telephone, whether your ex tries to talk to you on the pretense of calling your child, whether your ex tries to make visitation or other arrangements directly with your child, and whether you can afford the expense of a separate line and all the telephone calls that can be charged to it.

For those who can afford this luxury, it's not a bad idea. If you're going to do it, some ground rules should be set up so that fights don't develop between you and your ex and, even more important, between you and your child. Phone calls may be prohibited during certain hours, such as dinnertime, a designated homework period, and after bedtime. If your rules are not respected, the separate telephone number is history. Make sure *everyone* is clear about the rules.

Should my ex and I coordinate about gifts for important occasions in our children's lives and decisions concerning sports, camp, and school?

If you can, you should. It is wonderful when divorced parents can and do work together on these matters. The more children see their parents in unity, the more secure they feel. A unified approach is certainly more beneficial to the children, and a more productive use of money and time. It establishes some normalcy and continuity in a child's life. After all, what does a fourteen-year-old do when presented with two color televisions as a junior high school graduation gift? Or when soccer practice and golf lessons conflict on Saturday morning? Shouldn't Mom and Dad have spoken before Dad signed him up for golf and Mom signed him up for soccer at the same time?

Every small thing does not have to be discussed. But no matter what your relationship is with your ex, it's important there be some coordination concerning your children's activities and, to a lesser extent, gifts for various occasions.

Each of you should always provide the other with a copy of the children's schedules for school, camp, religious classes, and after-school activities. Whenever possible, discuss your child's enrollment in activities before signing up. If such discussions are impossible, maybe you can agree to divide responsibilities. Perhaps one parent should handle school and religious training, while the other handles enrollment in sports and extracurricular activities.

Your failure to coordinate at all with your former spouse can and probably will lead to confusion and anger on the part of your children when they suffer the consequences of your divorce interfering with their happiness. It's a small step from laughter to tears.

Put your differences aside for their benefit and talk about these things so that your children can have happy and normal lives.

Present a united front to your children on as many issues as possible.

United you stand; divided you may fall. Even with your differences, there are many things on which you and your former spouse should agree when it comes to the do's and don'ts for your kids. If you want your kids to do something—get better grades, stop skipping school, spend more time on homework, stay away from gangs at school, stop hitting a younger sibling, go to sleep on time—it's a lot easier to accomplish if there are two of you making the point. Parent-shopping to get a more favorable answer is an unfortunate by-product of divorce. Rules have more punch if children know that both parents support and enforce them. And as your children get older, more and more issues and conflicts will arise. An ally would be helpful to reinforce your position.

Support the other parent's rules and disciplinary decisions.

Don't undermine your former spouse when he or she sets rules for your child. If you do, and your spouse reciprocates, we guarantee anarchy. Children need to have structure and parameters. Although you may not want to be with your spouse, it's critical that both of you respect the rules you establish in your separate households.

Picture your child driving a car with all traffic lights, rules of the road, and signals removed. It becomes a nightmare of hit or miss. If you or your former spouse fails to respect the rules and discipline imposed on your children in your respective households, you are relegating your children to being raised without traffic lights, rules, and signals—an accident waiting to happen.

If you think this is overly dramatic, you're wrong. Your children are now living in two households rather than one. It's important that both places provide a stable, loving, and constructive environment for your children. If you take actions that undermine your former spouse's rules and handling of discipline or instill a lack of respect in your children for the way things are resolved in their other home, you will ultimately hurt your children. They will be confused and may end up not listening to either of you.

Share medical and educational information freely, including copies of report cards and notices and dates of school events.

If for even one tiny moment you have harbored the idea of not sharing this type of information with your spouse, you're wrong. Change your game plan immediately.

First, your former spouse has as much right to all this information as you do. Second, without the information he or she cannot always make sure your child is at the right place or doing what is necessary for school or some other project.

Last, the surest way to enrage a judge and risk changes to your custodial time with the children is to withhold information that your spouse has every right to have. It's not your information, it's your child's. Enough said.

Let your children take clothing, toys, books, and sports equipment back and forth freely between the two households.

It may come back dirty, ruined, with pieces missing, or not at all. Many parents have one of these retorts when the other parent suggests that their children be allowed to take things freely back and forth between households. Take the risk. It's not that great a risk, and the upside has real potential.

Just like adults, children often derive comfort from surrounding themselves with things they love, whether it's a favorite outfit, toy, book, or even a pillow. If it makes your children feel more comfortable and eases the transition from one home to another, let them take what they please. It's just stuff, far more replaceable than your child's happiness, self-esteem, and sense of well-being. Prohibiting them from taking these things with them may backfire.

Your children love you because you show them love. The parent with the most "toys" doesn't necessarily "win." Your children aren't going to love you more or want to be at your home simply because their special toys are there. You are more special than any toy.

When the children are with my ex, how do I handle it when my ex does things I don't approve of, such as:

- inappropriate behavior or language in front of the children;
- inappropriate movies and TV shows;
- dangerous activities such as dirt biking, skydiving, and flying in a small airplane.

We won't kid you; this can be a tough one. The best approach is usually the direct one. Try to talk to your spouse about the problem. See if the gentle art of persuasion can work. However, realistically, when the incidents are serious enough, it usually takes more than a conversation to resolve things.

One possibility is to set up in advance a neutral individual (lawyer, psychologist, clergy, friend) with whom you can both sit down and talk about these issues with an eye to resolution. Sometimes behavior will voluntarily be modified at the suggestion of a neutral party. Sometimes that same individual can facilitate a compromise. Of course, even voices of reason can fall on deaf ears.

Certainly a line must be drawn at dangerous activities, or activities that are dangerous given the age of the child. If your spouse allows your child to participate in a dangerous activity, you should try discussing it and getting an agreement never to do it again. But people may define "danger" differently. If you and your ex really can't agree on whether an activity is dangerous for your children, seek a court order prohibiting it. If your ex violates the court order, there are enforcement procedures, including jail, to deal with it.

One father suspected that his former wife's new husband was

an alcoholic, so he sought a restraining order to prevent his former wife from allowing their eight-year-old daughter to fly in a six-seater airplane piloted by her new spouse. The issue was ultimately settled by an agreement that their daughter would fly only on a commercial airplane.

There is still a giant gray area, however, where you and your spouse may simply have different ideas of what is appropriate. If you discuss your opinions and don't approach the subject with fault and blame, your ex may simply agree not to repeat the activity. If that's not the case, you should make your opinion and the reasons for it clear in writing.

When your child is with your ex, he or she controls many aspects of that child's life. Although you may not approve, there are many decisions that you just can't control. Certain disagreements about child-rearing are the call of the custodial parent, and there's nothing a court will do about it. It doesn't necessarily follow that you can substitute your rules for your spouse's. But if you feel that your child is at physical or emotional risk, and you haven't been able to reason with your ex, it will be necessary to contact an attorney and explore your remedies in court. Restraining orders prohibiting your former spouse from allowing the children to engage in certain type of activities can be obtained. Orders prohibiting specific language and behavior in front of the children can also be obtained. If your former spouse has stepped out of line, a request can be made to the court for him or her to contribute or pay the attorney's fees incurred in connection with obtaining these orders.

Don't shrug your shoulders in despair and let your ex get away with inappropriate or dangerous conduct. The system isn't perfect, but it can and will protect your children if you avail yourself of the opportunity to bring your position before a judge.

The best insurance is to teach your children what is appropriate and inappropriate. While it may be unfortunate that they receive poor guidance from their other parent, you can't control everything that happens when they're away from you.

What will happen when the children have vacations and holidays? Where will they go? Will I get to spend time with them?

It doesn't matter if it's a mother or father asking this question, the answer is the same. Yes, you will see them; some of the time they will be with you, and some of the time with your former spouse. But don't count on it turning out that way based on luck, faith, or the goodwill of your former spouse. *Holiday and vacation schedules should be spelled out in your divorce judgment with as much specificity as possible.*

The division of custodial time during holidays and vacations depends in large part on your normal day-to-day custodial arrangement and the physical distance between your homes. Naturally, the closer you live to each other, the easier it is for the children to go back and forth frequently. If you live in different states, however, or many hours apart in the same state, an appropriate schedule must be devised to reduce the amount of travel necessary.

Clear guidelines that define when the children are with each parent for vacations, holidays, and birthdays will give you and the children a more secure feeling. There should be a written schedule setting forth the times and dates when the children are to be with each of you. Normally, important holidays and extended vacations from school, such as Presidents' Day, Martin Luther King Day, spring or Easter break, Memorial Day, long weekends, Fourth of July, Labor Day, Halloween, Thanksgiving Day or the entire Thanksgiving weekend, winter or Christmas vacation, religious days, and any other holiday or vacation day that the family observes are alternated by year or divided between the parents.

Each parent should provide the other with an address and telephone number for contacting the child during extended vacations and holidays. The parent who is with the children should realize that the other parent is anxious about their welfare while they are on holiday. The parent who is not with the children should realize that it is important for them to have brief periods of uninterrupted time with the other parent, without interference.

Factors influencing the amount of time children spend with each parent in the summer include the following:

- If one parent lives out of the area and sees the children less frequently during the school year, he or she might have the children for a larger block of the summer.
- If the children are very young, it may be difficult for them to be away from their primary residence for extended periods of time.
- If one parent travels or has a work schedule that keeps him or her away from home a great deal, it may be impractical for the children to be at that home for extended periods.

During the summer, the children can alternate every week or every two weeks or even every three weeks with each parent. Many working parents find that two uninterrupted weeks in the summer is optimum; they can use their vacation days to spend time with their children.

The most important thing to keep in mind is that the custodial time for holidays and vacations should be discussed and resolved *before* your case is concluded. Make sure this time with your children is guaranteed to you in writing.

You can protect your children by considering your child's feelings and recognizing what you can do to ensure that these times are happy and enjoyable for your child.

Assert your rights for child support.

Children must eat, be clothed, have a place to live, go to school, and pursue activities. This requires money. The parent with whom they primarily live contributes to their support by providing, at a minimum, a place to live, clothes, and food. Child support is not a privilege; it's a court-ordered right. Both parents should contribute to support. If the parties can't agree, the court will determine the correct amount of support. If appropriate, the court will also make orders for medical insurance, dental insurance, payments for uninsured medical expenses, life insurance, private school, or activities.

Don't let intimidation or bullying scare you off. Stand up for your children and enforce your rights.

Don't hesitate to seek steps to enforce your rights if your spouse refuses to comply with court orders.

Don't throw your hands up and say you're tired of fighting. Court orders can be worth the paper they're written on if you assert your rights.

Do not let your spouse get away with withholding your visitation, not paying support to which you are entitled, or seeking in any manner to avoid or thwart rights that you have been given pursuant to a court order.

When you let your spouse get away with it once, it just leaves the door open for it to happen again and again. No one can stop you if you want to be a victim. The plain truth is you don't have to be. Courts usually deal severely with parties who substantially violate court orders. If the violation involves the non-payment of support, the district attorney's office, at no expense to you, will commence enforcement proceedings on your behalf. Certainly, you have the right to request payment of your attorney's fees incurred in connection with seeking compliance with existing court orders.

Do not let your former spouse intimidate you into giving up your rights. That may be a crime in and of itself. Bring any threats you may receive to the attention of your attorney and the court.

Without respect for court orders, the system has no meaning. Only you know if there is compliance with the orders. You aid your former spouse in undermining the integrity of the system when you fail to assert your rights.

Stick up for your rights. You're the protector of your children.

What do I do if I think my spouse is going to kidnap our children? Are there precautions I can take?

Paranoia, revenge, or reality? Make sure there's a rational basis for your fear of kidnapping. If there is, it's imperative that you take as many precautions as possible. However, your fear can not be a result of disliking or distrusting your ex. Every horrid former spouse is not a potential kidnapper.

If you believe that kidnapping is a genuine possibility but do not yet have evidence, the first step is to formally and legally establish that you have custody of your child. Be sure the order has a *specific* visitation or custody schedule spelled out for your spouse. Language that states "to be mutually agreed by the parties" is not good enough. If kidnapping is a real possibility, it's best to have restricted visitation—no overnights, infrequent visits, and contact for limited hours. If you have grounds that are persuasive, ideally your order includes what is known as monitored or supervised visitation. This means that an approved adult will be present at all times when your spouse visits with the children—in other words, a watchdog with the ability to talk, walk, and remove your children from harm's way.

Unfortunately, parents who fear abduction frequently don't have enough evidence to justify obtaining an order for limited visitation and a monitor. These are the parents who are truly terrified that a child could disappear at any moment. They are unable to convince the court that their fears have justification. If that is your case, make sure your court order includes these provisions:

- specific orders prohibiting the removal of the child from the city (or county or state) without written consent from the other parent or court order having first been obtained;
- an order that the non-custodial parent be required to post a bond to ensure that the child is returned at the end of the visitation period. This is necessary if there is a history of problems with custody. To obtain this order, you will need very convincing evidence;
- a clause in the judgment advising each parent of the penalties for child abduction;
- orders that require each parent to keep the other advised of the phone number and address where the child will be when that parent has custody, even for a day trip out of the area;
- mandates that you or the court will be the custodian of the children's passports.

There are many precautions you can take in your day-to-day activities, some of which include your children. Some suggestions:

- Emphasize to your children that you must always know the address and phone number where they are and where they will be.
- Make sure your children know how to call 911 and place a collect or credit card phone call to you or designated individuals whom they can call for help if abducted, even if they aren't carrying money.

- Check in frequently with your children or their caretaker when you are away from home. Mobile phones and beepers are handy devices to keep in touch with your children.
- Have a neighbor or close friend go to your house and check the children. Obtain a home security system or a dog or any other method by which you can make your home more secure.
- It may be wise for both you and your children to learn some forms of self-defense.
- Explain to your children when they will be seeing their other parent and make sure they understand that they are not to go with him or her except during those specific times.
- Make sure the children understand they are not to get on a plane, train, or bus for an unplanned trip.

Some of these precautions are almost routine. Some are very extreme and would not be recommended unless you are genuinely concerned about abduction. That is a call only you can make. All threats should be taken seriously. There are many more children abducted than one would imagine. It is a nightmare beyond description. If your child is abducted, there are many agencies that will help you, but that is of little comfort. If the threat is real, consider taking all the actions we have suggested and as many other courses of action as you or your attorney consider reasonable. You can never be too careful.

A NEW CHAPTER
The Best Is Yet to Come

Rekindle old friends and old interests.

Divorce—a time for "out with the old and in with the new." Nonetheless, there can be great satisfaction in renewing some old pleasures.

We all have friends with whom we loved to spend time but with whom we have lost contact. Maybe you haven't spoken to friends because you just didn't have the time during your marriage or they loathed your spouse. Did your spouse threaten to leave you if you wanted to spend an evening alone with old friends? Well, now you have the freedom and the time to see whomever you want and do whatever you want. Revisit your old passion for trains, crocheting, woodcarving, antique Japanese prints . . .

Moving ahead and rekindling old friendships and interests can be a satisfying blend.

Do what you can afford to make yourself feel good.

Feel good about *you*! Figure out what it takes.

A new beginning can only work if you start with a good attitude. Part of what shapes that attitude is how you feel about yourself.

For some it may be as easy as a new outfit or haircut. For others it may be finishing a degree, attending aerobics classes, fly-fishing, exploring a spiritual side, or simply hiking a trail or climbing a mountain that has challenged you for years.

Recognize that we all have different ways to feel attractive. Go out there and get in touch with what makes you feel good about you.

It's amazing what you can accomplish when you feel good.

Plan ahead financially.

Pull out your calculator. Turn on your computer. And no more "Tomorrow's another day." Obtain medical insurance, get credit in your own name, work out a budget, consult a financial planner, find less expensive places to shop, figure out how to make your money go further (but watch out for people who have the *greatest* place for you to invest your money). For accounting and tax advice, line up people who are well qualified and whom you trust.

Single people have to take financial responsibility. It's essential that you take the necessary steps on your behalf to ensure you are protected. If it's too difficult a task, find a competent and honest individual who can assist you with your financial planning, getting your bills paid, making sure your insurance is in place, and investing your assets prudently. There are people who do this for a living, but you'll have to pay them. You may be able to do it on our own; it just means taking the time to do the research.

Divorce leaves you with less than you had before, so make the necessary mental adjustments before you spend money you no longer have. Planning is the key. Think about ways you can save, and weigh the items on which you choose to spend money. Prioritize your expenses so that you have money for your real needs before you spend money on luxuries. If you need financial help, get it from a well-qualified professional who has your best interests in mind, someone who has no conflict of interest and nothing to sell you, someone who will not profit by your investment in a particular product. Interview several people and find a person with whom you feel comfortable and secure. Then listen carefully to make sure you're getting the kind of advice that is helpful to you in your particular situation.

None of us likes taking care of business. If it's one of those things you dread and avoid, set aside a certain number of hours on a designated day of the month for your bookkeeping, bill paying, and financial planning time.

Don't go looking to repeat old mistakes. Learn from your divorce about the kind of relationships you want, about how you can do it better next time, and what you want and don't want in a new relationship.

"If I knew then what I know now, I wouldn't have married my spouse." We've heard it a million times. So, learn from your mistakes. Figure out what you don't want or need as well as what you do want or need. Be realistic about your demands. Search your mind and heart about what you did right and what you did wrong. It's a way to avoid making the same mistakes again.

If your goal is to stay exactly the same, there's a good possibility that you'll find yourself back in the same mess you were in before.

Don't try to relive the past and don't blame yourself.

It's like a broken record playing the same song over and over again. It'll do you no good and drive you nuts.

The temptation to think about everything that went wrong, to play scenarios over and over again in your head, and to dwell on things you should have or could have done is not unusual. It's also counterproductive. What's the point?

Learn from your mistakes and get over them. Don't wallow in blame, guilt, and self-pity. Move ahead toward uncharted territories.

Don't isolate yourself.

Avoid the temptation to curl up into a fetal position, adopt a permanent pout, feel thoroughly sorry for yourself, and never leave the house. Not a very attractive picture, is it? But a lot of people do it anyway.

Get out and do things with people. It doesn't matter what you do as long as it keeps you remembering that you're still part of the human race. The more time you spend with people and the more you are involved with things other than your own problems, the more quickly you'll get back into the mainstream and start feeling whole again.

If you think there's nothing you feel up to doing, think again. The options are unlimited. Try some of these on for size:

- classes at the local university
- bridge groups
- networking executive groups
- tennis classes
- basketball for over thirtysomethings
- local theater groups (you don't need to act; you can type, do props, music, or even pull the curtains)
- wine-tasting events
- book clubs
- folk dancing
- health clubs

- library
- civic committees

Check with your temple, church, or city organizations for social events ranging from hiking or biking the mountains to singles parties. Don't overlook volunteer activities. Sometimes helping someone less fortunate than yourself can give you a whole new perspective on your troubles.

Throw out or give away objects that bum you out.
Admit it. You have that urge to hang on to certain objects that are guaranteed to reduce you to tears or, at the very least, conjure up painful memories.

If you look at "it" and "it" makes you cry, throw "it" out or give "it" away. Wait for one of your stronger moments, then trash it.

Last year's calendars with all the events you and your spouse celebrated should be discarded if they cause you distress. An old letter sweater or special perfume bottle that evokes memories you'd rather not revisit should be tossed at the first opportunity. Divorce is difficult enough without the trauma of seeing, feeling, and smelling emotionally charged objects that upset you. Why we hold on to these items is truly one of the mysteries of life, but all of us do. Don't use those objects as another excuse to wallow in misery. Give yourself a break and just toss them.

If needed, go to therapy to work out divorce-related problems.
It's difficult to start over and walk down a new aisle lugging three tons of old suitcases. Lose your baggage or at least minimize it to a carry-on bag. Virtually everyone who has been divorced has issues regarding their marriage. If you feel you need to discuss and resolve these issues, get help so you don't repeat your mistakes,

blame yourself endlessly, and spend the rest of your life with recriminations about a marriage that is over.

Just as it helps some people to seek therapy while going through the process, sometimes as much or more therapy is needed when the divorce is final.

In divorce we often talk about closure. Although that's everyone's goal, when reached it can seem empty and without great reward. It's not unusual to feel drained or angry or sad or just plain defeated. The relief most people expect to feel when it's over is frequently not forthcoming.

Talking to someone about your feelings can be helpful in starting over. It's a very personal and individual decision. Do what's right for you.

Don't mistake rebounding for love.

It's not like riding a bicycle. You don't have to jump right back on the minute you fall off!

Just because you want to fall in love again—just because you're ready to fall in love again—doesn't mean the first good-looking face or kind heart or fun-filled romantic night is love. It may be, but it may not.

Remember, you're vulnerable and perhaps a little needy. That combination can lead you to jump to conclusions and make hasty, regrettable decisions.

Don't settle for the quick fix engendered by feeling good because someone is treating you well, flattering you, and making you feel good. All those things are great, but they may or may not add up to love. So be sure to consider what you need and want in the long term and whether this new relationship can give it to you and keep giving it to you in the years to come. Like the Energizer bunny, you want love, years from now, to be "still going."

Your first consideration shouldn't be whether a job will reduce the support you receive or increase the support you pay. Do what's best for you in the long run.

This is the rest of your life, and you can't spend it worrying about how every decision impacts your divorce settlement. Sure it's smart to consider all your options, but when a good career opportunity comes along, your first consideration should be where it will take you professionally. The fact that it may mean you will receive less or more support should be of little consequence.

Letting considerations about support payments control career decisions is not only foolish but self-destructive. Accomplish what you can for yourself and let the other chips fall where they may.

Women can return to a prior name, but be sure to consider the effect on children of the marriage.

In most states, women can request the restoration of their maiden name or prior name. For some, particularly in short marriages, this can be a very nice and desired option. Even women in long marriages often make this request.

Children in divorced families are sensitive to conflicts. Some children will feel funny if their name is different from yours, while others really don't care. Schools and other institutions are frequently insensitive and oblivious to the pain caused by their questioning why a child's name is different from a parent's. Knowing this, and having considered your own child, you may still want to change or regain your name. You may change your name if you remarry. Before you do it, just be aware of the effect this may have on your child so that you can help your child make any adjustments.

Collect all your divorce papers and put them in a secure place to which you have access.

Although you might want to start a bonfire with all the papers, don't. As soon as the last glow disappears, count on needing one of those documents. On and off through the years you will need to refer to or produce copies of your final papers.

When you are reasonably sure the process has ended, put the documents away. As with other important papers of your life (car registration, deed to house, birth certificates, wills, and so on) you should put these papers in a safe place where they are accessible if you need them. Your options can range from a locked (and preferably fireproof) drawer or cabinet in your home to a safety deposit box.

When your divorce is over, make sure all the paperwork is organized so that you can find a particular document later if you need it. You may want to make a separate file that contains copies of your divorce judgment or other documents which contain orders on important points, such as custody or division of property, so you can refer to them easily or produce them as needed.

Just your luck! You finally found the person of your dreams. You're running down to City Hall for the marriage license, and you can't find your divorce papers. Aren't you going to kick yourself for not following our advice?

Try to avoid new conflicts with your ex.

The hardest way to move on with your life is to have new battles with an old enemy. Make every effort to avoid conflicts with your former spouse.

Maybe it's easier said than done, but try not to "engage" your former spouse in any conflict. If you can resolve it between you, fine. If not—and this point is important—involve your attorney. If it's not an important issue, forget about it, compromise, or just hope time resolves it. Fighting with your ex is one of the surest ways to make it difficult to start a new personal life, not to mention the adverse effect it has on your work, productivity, creativity, and, of course, your children.

Some former spouses may want to remain involved in your life and will do *anything* to stay involved with you. Don't let them. Let the divorce be a divorce. Eventually, most people will get the message and go their own way. You can help close the door by not continuing the involvement.

Diffuse matters before they escalate. Provided that you and your children are still protected, consider giving in even if you're right. We know that may be difficult, but don't lose sight of the fact that new conflicts may mean the need to rehire attorneys and add more expense, frustration, and turmoil. With that kind of aggravation to look forward to, giving in may look more attractive.

Enjoy the time with your children.
It's over and a time-sharing schedule is in place. Now sit back, take a breath, and enjoy your kids.

Whatever time you have with your children, enjoy it. They grow up fast, and in a blink, their childhood is over. Don't waste the time you have together bemoaning the fact that you don't have more time or different time. While they're with you, love them. It's the *quality* of time you have together that counts, not the quantity.

Think about new goals.
Because they may not necessarily be the same as your old goals. You're a recovering single person, formerly a married person. It's inevitable that you're going to be looking at everything a little differently now.

Take some time to think about what you want to do, what you

want to accomplish, where you want to go. A doctor's wife discovered after her divorce that staying home was not who she was. With wonderful energy and resolve, she enrolled in a professional chef's college and began the years of preparation needed to become a gourmet chef. *Bon appétit!*

Do you want to visit Italy instead of thinking about it as you have for the last fifteen years? Do you want to finally write, instead of talk about, the great American novel? Do you want to learn how to play chess? Move up to the next level in your company? Learn how to scuba dive? Wrestle alligators?

This is a new start. Sure, you carry some of the baggage of the past, but it's not a load that should weigh you down. Explore your options. Consider the possibilities.

Where would you like to be one year from today? Give that some thought, pack new bags, and start on the road to take you there.